The Warhol Initiative.
Capacity-building in the Visual Arts

The Warhol Initiative.
Capacity-building in the Visual Arts

I first encountered the extraordinary group of visual arts organizations known as alternative spaces when I began working at the foundation many years ago. Though I was familiar with some of New York City's better-known alternative spaces, I had no idea of the richness and breadth of the nationwide network of these artist-founded and artist-centered organizations. Small and intimate, often run on shoestring budgets, and bearing strongly the marks of the visions and personalities of their creators, these groups have made a tremendous impression upon me over the years. I well remember how, back in the 1980s, they were among the first to grapple publicly with the AIDS crisis, presenting work by artists about the disease and the devastation it was wreaking on their communities. Audiences were also likely to see thought-provoking political work, or to encounter unflinching representations of sexuality. Then as now, alternative spaces did not shy away from controversy, and their small, local, individual natures often gave them more freedom to express their own particular visions than larger institutions. Because a founding principle for most was to be true to the needs and values of contemporary artists, they championed artists even when their work generated bitter political attacks. They also became important platforms for artists who might never have received public exposure without them—women, minorities, others who in earlier generations had difficulty making their voices heard.

At the same time as they have played this important social role, they have, most centrally, been the incubators of the culturally and aesthetically new, the progressive, the cutting-edge. They are laboratories for artistic expression, and, with their flexibility and openness to novelty and change, present the kinds of artistic experimentation that can break new ground for an artist, a medium, even a field. They discover and are the first to show artists who later turn up in major museums or win international acclaim; they also provide a home for local artists who may never show outside of their own communities. Alternative spaces have been pursuing these activities for years, enabled by their dedicated leaders, board members and staffs – all of whom work long hours and whose greatest reward is the knowledge that they are furthering the cause of contemporary art and artists. Every year they are joined by a few newly-created organizations like them, who come to the difficult struggle of supporting artists and enabling the creation of contemporary art with a fresh drive and new hopes and goals. Together the older- and younger-generation contemporary art spaces are performing a tremendous service to the country. By serving young, unknown, or marginalized artists, by being unafraid to present work that is experimental or has challenging content, they occupy a critically important spot on the cultural landscape, one that has never been filled by any other type of arts organization. This report is the record of one foundation's effort to strengthen and encourage these alternative spaces – in order that they, in turn, can do the same for the artists they serve.

Pamela Clapp, Program Director

Andy Warhol
Art, c. 1985–86
Synthetic polymer paint
and silkscreen ink on canvas
16 x 20 inches

<u>Setting the Context</u>. In the fall of 1999, the Andy Warhol Foundation for the Visual Arts launched an ambitious project in support of small contemporary visual arts organizations around the country. The Warhol Initiative offered local arts groups with strong visual art programs large grants of about one hundred and twenty-five thousand dollars each, along with consulting services to help them maximize the grants' benefits. The venture's goal was to help groups gain a more stable financial footing and improve their service to artists. With significant funds in the bank, recipients were able to undertake long-term financial planning and then embark on efforts to strengthen their future prospects. The arts groups began a variety of projects: improving their technological resources, addressing urgent facilities issues, creating cash reserves to allow for more efficient fiscal management. They worked with consultants on management issues, staff and board development, and strategies for increasing revenue. As an additional support for these efforts, the foundation sponsored biennial conferences at which the organizations' directors and board chairs met their peers and participated in workshops and consultant-led training sessions. During the first five years of the program – the first of a planned two phases – its grantees showed signifi-cant increases in organizational capacity, and most made strong progress towards greater financial stability.

Anton Perich
<u>Untitled</u>, 1979
Black and white print
8 x 10 inches

Through the Initiative, the Warhol Foundation has already served thirty-one contemporary visual arts organizations, helping them towards more secure futures in today's difficult economic and cultural environment. This report describes the Initiative: how it came into being, was carried out, and – to the best of our understanding – what its impact has been thus far on the organizations it has served. It is the foundation's hope that the report may assist and even inspire other similar efforts, whether in the arts or in other fields. Progressive, adventurous, forward-thinking groups like the program's grantees are on the front lines of service to their constituencies, providing assistance where it is most needed. The Initiative's work is critical for the future of its grantees; and they and others like them are essential to our nation's cultural health and well-being. At five million dollars over five years with a three million dollar second phase beginning in 2004, the Warhol Initiative has been, financially speaking, a relatively small venture, but it has been a successful and, we believe, an important one.

About the foundation. The Andy Warhol Foundation was created in 1987, upon the death of the great artist who was its founder. When Warhol died unexpectedly at the age of 58, he left his estate to create a foundation "dedicated to the advancement of the visual arts." The interpretation of this broad directive became the task of the professional board formed to realize the founder's vision. The board decided that although the foundation would give exclusively to non-profit arts organizations, Warhol the artist would be its guiding spirit, and the foundation's grantmaking would be carried out with the needs and interests of the creative individual always foremost.

For the foundation's directors and staff, that meant that small to moderate-size contemporary visual arts organizations would be at the heart of its mission and activities. They saw that "artist-centered" groups were the ones at work supporting artists on the ground in local communities. Often more regional than national in their orientation, these groups kept in close touch with the artists in their communities, discovered them, presented them, and provided them with many essential supports, from professional development services to first critical assessments. They became gathering places for artists, exhibited work that inspired them, and connected them with other artists and with audiences. In short, though their primary mission was simply to present contemporary art, these groups, in carrying it out, essentially became service organizations for artists and today provide much of the support that is currently available to American artists.

Unfortunately, however, these kinds of small non-profits are among the most endangered of American arts organizations. Important as contemporary art spaces are to the ecosystem of the visual arts, historically, their financial support has been among the lowest of all philanthropic giving. A 2004 *Grantmakers in the Arts* study of giving by more than 1,000 foundations ranked the visual arts last among all types of arts and culture philanthropy. Indeed, according to the study, in 2002, foundation support for the visual arts represented only four percent of all arts and culture grants, declining from seven percent in 2001. Contemporary visual arts organizations had also experienced a significant contraction in funds available from local, state and federal government, which had historically been a crucial source for them. Many were founded during an era of more generous public funding (a significant number in the '70s and '80s, when such support for the arts was at its peak); with these sources in steep decline, and private funding also increasingly difficult to obtain, many groups have struggled to survive – and not all have succeeded. Often guided by either explicit or implicit progressive political agendas, many have also run afoul of today's polarized cultural environment.

By 1998, the Warhol Foundation's staff and board had been following these organizations closely for over a decade and had become increasingly aware of the challenges they faced. While the foundation had always given generously to such groups, its "project grants" (funds directed towards discrete programming events) could only be spent on the specific exhibit, residency or other project they funded. The more the foundation studied its constituency of small contemporary arts organizations, the more it realized that a different kind of help was also needed, and in 1999, it commissioned a non-profit management company, the LarsonAllen Public Service Group, to conduct a study of the types of support available to small to mid-size visual arts organizations. To no one's surprise, the results showed a chronic shortage of resources for these groups, and a particularly dramatic drop-off in available money in the wake of the culture wars of the 1990s with their resultant changes in the National Endowment for the Arts. After much discussion of the difficulties both the study and its own experience confirmed, the foundation's board asked its staff to articulate a new program that would address in a comprehensive manner the issues facing these contemporary arts groups. And so the Initiative was born.

Capacity-building

The first question that confronted the foundation as it began to consider the new project was how best to design a program that would help small visual arts organizations achieve greater stability to better carry out their missions. The simplest option – adding general operating support grants to the foundation's program – was discussed but quickly set aside in favor of a more comprehensive effort. For the more the foundation considered the critical financial environment and the historic underdevelopment of the visual arts field, the clearer it became that an intensive, concentrated approach to addressing the needs of this group was required. To design the program, the foundation put together a team consisting of its own program staff, Pamela Clapp and Yona Backer, and an advisory panel made up of two arts professionals, Jennifer Dowley and Helen Brunner, as well as two experts in non-profit management, Susan Kenny Stevens and Susan Moore, both of LarsonAllen. The panel concluded that the best approach was a capacity-building project and set out to design one that would be particularly suited to the needs of this constituency.

Capacity-building defined. In the parlance of non-profit management, "capacity" is an important word. It denotes organizational capability and competence and is generally used in reference to the operational and financial components of non-profit work – the supporting infrastructure that assures the quality and sustainable continuance of a non-profit's mission, program and other services. As such, capacity-building projects sometimes seem arduous, unglamorous, or of only limited value; they address an organization's mission not directly but indirectly, helping the group to carry out its primary work only by strengthening the infrastructure that enables its programming. Yet there are few things that more effectively enhance an

Andy Warhol
Little Race Riot, 1964
Silkscreen ink on synthetic polymer paint on canvas
30 x 33 inches each panel

organization's long-term viability and ability to do high-quality work than improving its organizational functioning. In the service of this goal, capacity-building projects address staffing issues, housing questions, and technology. They aim to improve board function and board-staff interaction, as well as financial management and marketing. The theory behind capacity-building projects is that a healthy, well-run and fiscally sound organization is best positioned to fulfill its mission effectively and to present the highest quality programming.

Over the past decade, many national and local foundations have adopted capacity-building grant programs to help strengthen the financial and operating structures of important grantees. The programs take different forms and have different emphases, but they tend to include at least two of the following three components: a substantial monetary investment; individualized technical assistance provided by outside consultants; and peer-group programming. How these program elements combine and which are most prominent depend upon the foundation's own program goals and financial capabilities. Following are some different types of capacity-building efforts.

Some capacity programs are *performance-based*. In projects like these, the donor organization articulates specific desired outcomes at the beginning of the effort; the grant money is paid out only if these goals are achieved. As a general rule, the targets in these cases are financial ones: increase earned income by a certain percentage; decrease debt, etc. Participants receive technical assistance and may engage in peer activities, but the focus tends to be on measurably improved financial and operational performance, and grant money is withheld if specific goals are not met.

Other capacity programs make *operating support* investments that supplement the annual income of particular grantees. Usually designed as long-term projects for grantees whose missions are well-aligned with those of the foundation, these efforts emphasize individual and group technical assistance as the focal point for organizational improvement. Although progress towards specific goals may be evaluated, financial awards are not generally contingent upon performance. The issue with ongoing support for operating expenses, however, is that it can cause serious difficulties for an organization when funds they have come to depend on to function are withdrawn when the project terminates.

Endowment-building is yet another capacity-building strategy, one of the earliest types to come into regular use. Although it can still be an excellent tool for strengthening the capitalization of mature organizations or those with sufficient operating income and working capital reserves, in many cases, endowments have proven to be too restrictive for small and mid-size organizations. These groups may have financial needs that fluctuate from month to month, and putting aside large sums of capital that cannot be touched is often not the most helpful way to allocate such a significant portion of an organization's resources.

A fourth capacity-building strategy tries to combine the merits of the others. It aims at improving non-profits' underdeveloped financial *capitalization*. Here, a sizable grant is offered, accompanied, as usual, by technical assistance and peer engagement opportunities. As in an endowment-building project, the financial award is intended to boost an organization's overall net worth rather than fund its annual operating budget, but in this case it is offered with a flexibility that allows the recipient to decide, usually in consultation with technical advisors, how to allocate the funds. Some of the money may be used for specific, one-time only projects, like upgrading technology or paying off a mortgage, but often much of it is put into "cash reserves." These are unrestricted funds which are set aside for future strategic opportunities. Sizable chunks of capital that do not service an organization's ordinary operational requirements, they can make money work for the organization the way an endowment fund would, but also allow funds to be accessible when needed. There are different ways for an organization to handle the relative restrictedness or availability of these funds. Some boards adopt an "untouchable" policy with their reserves, viewing them as quasi-endowments that may be drawn upon only under exceptional circumstances. Others allow portions of the reserve to act as an internal line of credit that can even out temporary cash flow problems. Still others strategically invest portions of their reserves in high-impact activities that have the potential to increase operating income in the future; for example, earned income activities, or paying off high-interest mortgages. But whatever the details of their use, they are employed strategically to serve an organization's specific needs, and have the overall effect of increasing a non-profit's net worth. The one thing they do not do is provide ongoing operating support; they are not used for operational purposes and except under unique circumstances do not fund staff positions or other sustained operating expenses.

Dr. Susan Kenny Stevens, director of LarsonAllen Public Service Group and a member of the foundation's advisory panel, consulted with the foundation on the program's design and was a strong proponent of this approach to capacity-building. For her, strengthening non-profit capitalization, though not perhaps the most common capacity-building strategy, is nevertheless one of the best. Such an approach acknowledges the needs complex and growing organizations have for flexible, unrestricted capital that exists outside of the budget's parameters, and takes into account the fact that the majority of arts organizations, and small and mid-size visual arts groups in particular, have been historically undercapitalized. Stevens had previously developed the *Cash Reserve for the Arts Program* as well as numerous other capacity-building programs for national and local foundations, and she had significant experience in building successful projects like this one.

For Stevens, sustainable capacity programs start with the primacy of organizational mission, constituency, and programming. Self-evident as this may seem, the time and energy capacity-building activities require around non-program areas such as board development, upgrading financial systems, and creating more sustainable revenue structures can make organizational capacity seem like a driver, rather than simply a support mechanism for mission sustainability. While it is essential to focus intently on these efforts, the organization must never lose track of its true goal: serving its mission and constituency. Secondly, sustainable capacity programs are holistic; they usually affect nearly every aspect of an organization's functioning and decision-making. Consequently, in the process of building capacity, organizations nearly always undergo a series of internal changes in their actions, their thought patterns and ultimately their behavior. These changes can and will threaten the status quo; they need to be anticipated and managed skillfully by program consultants, program officers, and constituents.

Like all growing pains, upsets to the status quo can be quite uncomfortable at the outset. Yet they are a normal and predictable part of the capacity-building process and must be addressed as such. Finally, and this is fundamental to sustainable capacity-building, organizations that "internalize" capacity changes – take them to heart and make them their own – are the ones that are most likely to sustain improvements over time. Programs perceived as imposed from the outside, or as not developing organically out of a group's own needs and desires, are less likely to receive participants' full buy-in, and therefore may not create the sustainable habits that will enable permanent beneficial change.

With these thoughts in mind, the Warhol Foundation set out to design a capacity-building program that would build on each organization's unique service to artists; strengthen its overall organizational and financial platform both now and in the future; and do both while making sure that the program would be flexible and sensitive enough to respond to the individual character, needs and challenges of each group.

Program Design
This section presents the Warhol Initiative's program – the nuts and bolts of how the project actually worked. It describes the three primary grant instruments the foundation used to enhance the grantees' financial and operating capacity: capitalization grants of approximately $125,000; small technical assistance awards to support basic in-house knowledge and technical capacity, and biennial peer convenings that created connections among the groups and helped them to share their hard-won knowledge with each other.

Eligibility, application and selection process. At the beginning of each year, the Initiative's advisory panel – Pamela Clapp, Yona Backer, Helen Brunner, Jennifer Dowley, Susan Kenny Stevens and Susan Moore – met to create a list of eligible organizations that would be invited to apply to the program. At a second meeting they selected the seven to nine grantees for that year; over the course of the four years, a total of thirty-one were chosen for the first phase, and in 2004, another twelve were added for the Initiative's second phase. The criteria for selection were a demonstrated track-record of strong artist-centered programming, along with an organizational dedication to supporting artists' professional growth and development. In addition to these programming criteria, the foundation chose organizations with annual operating budgets under one million dollars; leadership able and eager to embrace a creative approach to achieving organizational potential; and infrastructure requirements consistent with the resources of the program.

An invitation was sent to each group describing the Initiative and expressing the foundation's desire to assist artist-centered organizations. Invitees were asked to submit a short letter of application discussing how the group's acceptance into the program would strengthen its support of artists, evaluating current financial and operating structures, and describing the types of financial and technical support that would allow it to more fully realize its potential. Detailed financial information on the applicants was also requested so that their fiscal status could be evaluated; the foundation wished to assist those who truly needed help, but also wanted to ensure that all participants already had at least a modicum of fiscal stability. All applicants received a stipend of $1,000 to make sure that the time and effort invested in the application would not be simply another drain on their already limited resources. When all the applications and financial materials had been received, the Initiative advisory committee met again to discuss each group in detail and to select that year's grantees.

Facilitated self-assessments. Once the participants were selected, the first order of business was to obtain a comprehensive picture of their capabilities and needs and the challenges that confronted them. To accomplish this, each group would meet with a consultant to conduct a "facilitated self-assessment," in which board, staff and consultant would work together to develop a picture of its organizational, fiscal, strategic and programmatic status.

The facilitated self-assessments were designed following a paradigm developed by Stevens over the course of her work on capacity-building projects. Entitled the "lifecycle capacity model," and described in her book, *Nonprofit Lifecycles: Stage-based Wisdom for Nonprofit Capacity,* (Long Lake, MN: Stagewise Enterprises Inc., 2001), the paradigm posits seven stages of an organization's development, each of which involves a set of goals and challenges that are specific to that stage. During the *start-up years*, for example, an organization's principal task is to make its presence and services known in the marketplace; in the *growth stage*, by contrast, demand for the services is already well-established, but operating capacity limitations may reduce its ability to carry out its mission. Once an organization identifies where it is located on the lifecycle chart, it gains a clearer perspective on the types of issues it is likely to be facing (see sidebar page 10).

The key element of the lifecycle model is its vision of capacity as a set of shifting capabilities that are assessed in relation to an organization's lifecycle stage. In this view, a group's capacity is not a fixed set of achievements but is instead defined by its ability to meet the challenges posed by its lifecycle stage. The lifecycle model is intended to encourage self-analysis and self-direction among participants so that capacity-building supports can be strategically targeted; it also aims to help groups create roadmaps for achieving their future goals.

With the lifecycle model in hand, the groups embarked upon their self-assessments. A trained facilitator, the consultant, met with up to ten key staff and board leaders in a single long session. The facilitator, who had reviewed the organization's financial documents carefully beforehand, brought to the meeting both her in-depth engagement with the organization's particular fiscal situation and a professional's knowledge of the standards and expectations for non-profit financial management. Thus a group's fiscal health was a key component of this important conversation, which also covered many other topics, from overall organizational goals to current board and management challenges. As one participant said of the self-assessment, "The process prompted our board and staff to examine areas of our organizational structure and programming that, to our detriment, we might have otherwise missed."

The aim of the assessments was to enable the foundation and the grantees to come up with a mutually agreed-upon set of goals for the Initiative, and to give both a benchmark by which progress could be measured. The assessments also provided a comprehensive analysis of each individual organization and a snapshot of the kinds of challenges these groups experience collectively. The foundation now had an overarching picture of the context in which it offered

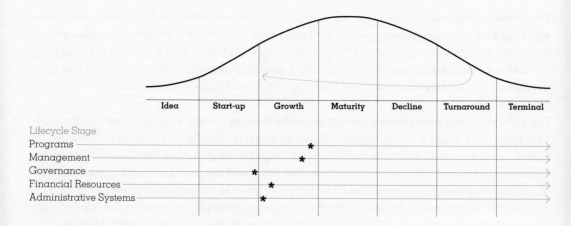

Idea	Start-up	Growth	Maturity	Decline	Turnaround	Terminal

Lifecycle Stage
Programs ————————————————————————— * ————→
Management ——————————————————————— * ————→
Governance ——————————— * ————————————————→
Financial Resources —————— * ——————————————→
Administrative Systems —— * ————————————————→

Stage 1: Idea.
The stage in which there is no formal organization, only an idea and a personal mandate to fill a societal, programmatic or cultural gap in the community.

Stage 2: Start-Up.
The beginning stage of organizational operations in which unbridled mission, energy, and passion reign supreme, but, generally, without corresponding governance, management, resources, or systems.

Stage 3: Growth.
The stage in which non-profit mission and programs have taken hold in the marketplace, but where service demand exceeds current structural and resource capabilities.

Stage 4: Maturity.
The stage of operation in which the organization is well-established, operating smoothly, and has a community reputation for providing consistently useful and high quality services.

Stage 5: Decline.
The stage in which the organization's services are no longer relevant to the marketplace, status-quo decisions are made, and declining program census creates insufficient operating income to cover expenses.

Stage 6: Turnaround.
The stage at which an organization, having faced a critical juncture due to lost market share and revenues, takes decisive action to reverse prior actions in a self-aware, determined manner.

Stage 7: Terminal.
The stage when an organization hasn't the will, purpose or energy to continue to exist.

its service, as well as a blueprint for how to design each individual capitalization and technical assistance grant. More importantly, as the following comment suggests, participants found the assessment process to be among the most valuable of the Initiative's components. "The self-assessment was the most helpful aspect of the Initiative. It brought staff and board closer together in critical debates about the organization – our mission and practices. We appreciated the assistance of an external advisor who brought fresh ideas and approaches to the table."

Following the assessment process, the facilitator drafted a report outlining the assessment's conclusions. The report also included initial recommendations for the use of Warhol technical assistance and grant funds. Although the goal of the assessment process was to develop consensus about the organization's situation, the reports did reflect the meetings as they had actually unfolded, and universal agreement was not always the only outcome. Thus both the assessments and the reports that documented them accommodated and recorded individual opinion, even as they worked towards agreement on the largest issues. Overall, participants found the assessments to be effective at generating consensus; as one grantee commented, "The guided self-assessment was incredibly helpful and got us all on the same page."

Technical assistance grants. Early on in the invitation and self-assessment process, the foundation realized that to take full advantage of the capitalization grants, many groups would require specific technical assistance to supplement their current knowledge; it also wanted to make sure they had the ability to make the best possible use of their cash grants. This was the logic behind the technical assistance component; and any grantee intending to use the capital infusion grants as a cash-reserve fund also received special financial training on how to appropriately account for, borrow from, and repay the reserve.

These initial $10,000 technical assistance grants were used to hire consultants to upgrade financial accounting and reporting systems; to assist with board development; to create business plans and set future direction; for the cash reserve training; and for marketing and audience development. As one group said of the technical assistance component, "The Initiative offered us an invaluable opportunity to receive consulting advice we could have never afforded. We have benefited enormously from the suggestions that will serve us in the near and the longer term."

Participants selected and hired their own consultants, which proved to be a learning experience for many of them. In a field where money is generally in short supply, most Initiative members had never retained a consultant. Perhaps as a result of this inexperience, when the Initiative conducted its annual evaluations, technical assistance was the one category that received the most uneven "benefit" marks. Although most felt it to be useful, for a few their initial experience with technical assistance was a disappointment. Yet when participants were invited to apply for supplemental capacity-building grants in 2004–5, more than 50 percent of them chose to spend the additional $15,000–$25,000 they received on consulting. Thus, despite some initial problems with the consultant services, we conclude that overall the Initiative participants did find the technical assistance grants to be of significant value.

Capitalization grants. The centerpiece of the Warhol Initiative was, of course, the $125,000 capitalization grant awarded to each organization with the aim of strengthening its overall financial condition. Most Initiative participants, as we have noted, used these working capital grants to establish or increase cash reserves. However a few paid down high-interest mortgages (and thus increased their day-to-day cash flow), or invested in activities that strengthened their financial value in different ways. For many of these frequently cash-strapped organizations, having the working capital to pay bills on time created a sense of security and fiscal health that was a new and positive experience.

The Initiative had another, less tangible effect upon its participants: having money in the bank and a strong plan for how to make use of it allowed them to begin thinking long-term about their organizations' futures. Suddenly groups that hadn't been sure they would be able to meet the next payroll felt confident planning for their organization's development in the years to come. As one group reported, "Knowing that someone believed in us enough to invest $125,000 in our long-term future really made our board and staff start thinking about the long-term rather than wondering just how we will get by year to year." Added another, "The cash reserve grant was a dream come true ... It allowed us to put long-range plans into effect, but the more immediate effect was that we adopted a new attitude about going forward." Indeed, as beneficial as the money was to their financial net worth, it was almost as significant in its ability to change staff and board members' visions of their organizations' potential. This in turn led to an overall growth in confidence that we see as one of the Initiative's greatest benefits.

The foundation encouraged participants to be flexible in their use of capitalization funds, tailoring their usage to the working capital issues identified in their self-assessments. Yet, knowing that many of these groups had never had significant "extra cash" before, it did put two important safeguards in place to ensure that funds would be used as semi-permanent capital rather than operating support: the cash reserves training mentioned above, and a simple contract detailing how funds would be used and under what circumstances they could be drawn upon.

Biennial retreats. In the Initiative's second, fourth and sixth years, the foundation invited the board chairs and directors of the grantee groups to weekend retreats, the first in Puerto Rico in 2001, the second in Miami in 2003, and the third in Los Angeles in 2005. Designed primarily to allow the leaders of the organizations to meet, engage with, and learn from each other, the retreats featured panels, roundtable discussions with peers, and sessions with non-profit management consultants on issues of significance to the groups. Questionnaires sent out in the months before the retreats asked for input on subjects of interest to the participants; the answers were then used to select the topics for the weekend's discussions. Each group also was given time to make a brief presentation about itself, its history and its programming. The sites of the retreats were chosen for their cultural richness and each weekend featured outings to museums, galleries, and private collections. The aim was to provide a fun and relaxing experience for these busy arts professionals, while still offering a full menu of profes-sional supports and engagements. Participants found the opportunity to meet their far-flung peers to be one of the retreat's most significant benefits; as one said, "It's great having the opportunity to convene with my peers in the field. They are such dedicated, hard-working and creative people. Since we don't have an organizing national entity for convenings, I found this to be the most important part of the retreat."

The structure of the retreats changed over the course of the program to reflect the participants' reactions to them. Although the initial impulse was to get as much hard content in as possible, and thus to rely heavily on consultants for technical instruction in management issues, in the second year the foundation realized that some of people's best experiences at the conferences came from talking and sharing with their peers. As a result, the second conference featured more participant-led panel discussions, roundtables and participant-selected topics. Balancing the desire for peer connection while still providing leave-behind information, particularly to content-hungry board members, was a continual planning tension. A typical comment suggests both the value of the experience and its limitations for participants: "I enjoyed the retreat tremendously... my only frustration was that the breakout session and workshops felt too short. It was hard to go beyond scratching the surface in the allotted time."

Overall, the feedback from those who attended the three retreats suggests that they were helpful and satisfying for the participants. While the foundation made some organizational changes from the first to the second meeting, and still sees room for improvement, participant comments indicate that overall the retreats had the effect their organizers had hoped for. "An incredible experience and of true value to us," said one; "we brought back many ideas and fresh approaches to the staff that were unable to attend. The support and shared ideas will continue well after the retreat."

THE PRINCETON Leader

First Weekly Newspaper in Kentucky To Be Granted Associated Press Membership

Volume 85 — PRINCETON, Caldwell County, Kentucky, Thursday, August 23, 1956

Native To Head Cairo, Egypt, Botany Department

Dr. ALTON M HARVILL SON of Mr and Mrs A.M. Harvill, of the Eddyville Road, will sail Friday AUGUST 24, from New York aboard the Ss. Exeter for Egypt where he will be head of the botany department at the The American university at Cairo

One of the nations fore most authorities on ARCTIC mosses, Dr HARVILL was in ALASKA as a bacteriologist and bio-chemist in The ARMY Medical CORPS during WORLD WAR II. He has published "A Phytogeographic STUDY ON A LASKA MOSSES", a paper ON the Aleutians and other works on the ARCTIC.

DR. HARVILL was in LIBERIA WEST AFRICA FROM 1953-1955. while he did research for The FIRESTONE Plantation laboratory ies at Harbel. He left there in 1955 and Toured Europe For three months

Before he returning to The STATES He went from the University of ALABAMA at TUSCA LOOSA in 1948 as a botanist, After getting The Ph.D. FROM THE University of Michigan He did his under graduate and graduate work at the University of KENTUCKY.

UNDERGOES SURGERY
BILL PRICE, SON OF MR and MRS HENRY PRICE, of the country, underwent surgery at the BAPTIST HOSPITAL AT NASHVILLE TUESDAY

Playground To be Open Next Summer

Youth incorporated HAS BALANCE OF $489, NO BILLS OUTSTANDING

The opening of Youth Incorporated's new playground, located off the Cadiz Road, will be held next year, it was announced this week.

Work on the present has been going on intermittently all summer and is expected to be completed next summer Already the field For THE TH LITTLE and Pony leagues has been graded, The dug outs have been erected, all Dent poles are up except one and the poles for the fence have been set. A base of crushed stone for asphalt-tennis courts is down and The courts are to be ready For play next summer.

MISS TRAVIS Graduates from SCHOOL OF NURSING

Miss BETTY RUTH TRAVIS, daughter of MR. and MRS. HARVIL 4 TRAVIS, Hopkinsville Road, graduated from the GOOD SAMARITAN SCHOOL OF NURSING at LEXINGTON last weekend. She will assume the duties as a SURGICAL Hospital at LEXINGTON on OCTOBER 1.

MR AND MRS TRAVIS AND SON ARTHUR were in LEXINGTON TO ATTEND the GRADUATION EXERCISES

GROWS WAIST HIGH DARK-FIRED TOBACCO: J.J. TANDY is shown standing here in an acre of WAIST HIGH dark-fired TOBACCO which he planted and cultivated all by himself this summer at the age of 78

Little League Pennant is won by Rotary Reds

The 1956 pennant winner of the little league baseball is the Rotary Reds, sponsored by the Princeton Rotary Club and managed by GLOVER LEWIS, JR. and Lowell Hobby.

Press Box To Be Built At The Butler Stadium

The Caldwell County School Board last week approved construction of a press box for newspaper and radio representatives on the west side of Butler Stadium.

Material to construct the press box, which will be above and behind seats on the west side of the stadium, will be donated by Gray Lumber Co., Kentucky by Products Co., Princeton Lumber Co., R. Robertson Lumber Co. The eight by 18 foot building will be on a concrete base.

Local Man Completets Apprenticeship As A Plumber, Steam Fitter

Charles A. LISANBY, an employee at B.N. Lusby Co., recently received a certificate of completion of apprenticeship as a plumber and steam fitter from The Kentucky Apprenticeship Council.

A message prepared by the secretary of Labor, JAMES P. MITCHELL, and forwarded to Oliver by the Louisville office of the Bureau of Apprenticeship said:

"Congratulations to you on the completion of your apprentice ship. I am sure that this training will bring you a lifetime of personal satisfaction....

"The Nation's need for well trained men and women in today's world is insatiable. Upon you, as journeymen, the nation must rely to train other men and women in the skilled crafts. I hope, therefore, that you will always strive to stimulate programs for the development of skilled workers in your local communities. As craftsmen, you have an obligation to pass on to others the value of training not only to the individual, but to the community and nation as well."

Andy Warhol
The Princeton Leader, c. 1956
Blue ballpoint on manila paper
16¾ x 13⅞ inches

1. Forty-three contemporary visual arts organizations were invited to apply to the Initiative; thirty-one were selected in four separate classes of about eight participants each. A second phase beginning in 2004, adds twelve more recently founded groups to the project. Each of these groups was well-known to the foundation for its artist-centered approach, and all had strong track records for artistic programming and service to their communities.

2. Once selected, each organization participated in a guided self-assessment in which key board and staff representatives took a critical look at their organizational strengths and challenges and how the Initiative's funds could best be used to financially strengthen the organization's ability to serve artists over the long term.

3. Each group received approximately $125,000, which most directed toward establishing or strengthening cash reserves, facilities-related projects, and upgrading technology.

4. Each group also received $10,000 technical assistance grants for capacity-building projects such as business planning, board development, and cash reserve training.

5. The Initiative also sponsored three weekend retreats – in Puerto Rico, Miami and Los Angeles – which brought together the directors and board chairs of each participating organization for peer learning, seminars, roundtable and panel discussions.

Warhol Initiative Participants. Phase One

Aljira, A Center for Contemporary Art Newark
Art in General New York
Artists Space New York
Atlanta Contemporary Art Center
Center for Women and Their Work Austin
CEPA Gallery Buffalo
Creative Time, Inc. New York
Dieu Donné Papermill New York
DiverseWorks Houston
Exit Art New York
509 Cultural Center aka The Luggage Store San Francisco
Galería de la Raza San Francisco
Hallwalls Contemporary Arts Center Buffalo
Headlands Center for the Arts Sausalito
Intermedia Arts Minneapolis
Kansas City Artists Coalition
Legion Arts Cedar Rapids
Los Angeles Contemporary Exhibitions
MACLA/Movimiento de Arte y Cultura Latino Americana San José
New Langton Arts San Francisco
911 Media Arts Center Seattle
Out North Anchorage
Project Row Houses Houston
Real Art Ways Hartford
Salina Art Center
SF Camerawork San Francisco
Self-Help Graphics & Art Los Angeles
Southern Exposure San Francisco
Space One Eleven Birmingham
SPACES Cleveland
White Columns New York

One of the most important features of the Initiative's design was that numerous mechanisms were built into it to provide feedback to the foundation from the grantees. The questionnaires, self-assessments, and other components, as well as open communication lines between grantees, foundation and technical advisors, had two parallel aims: first, the foundation wanted to make sure that its process could change and adapt in response to grantees' experience; second, it wanted to gain a comprehensive picture of the field, including organizations' financial data, management strategies, fiscal and other challenges, so that it could continue to provide ever more effective service. This portion of the report details the findings that were gathered over the course of the Initiative, and offers some suggestions about how best to address the issues and challenges they raise.

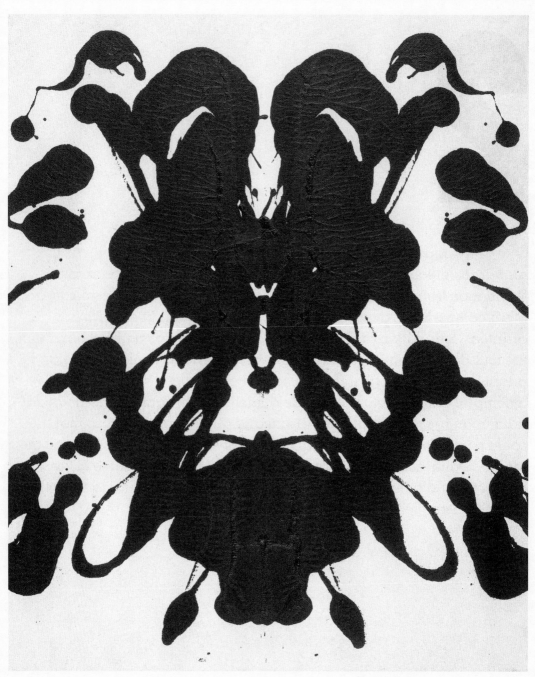

Andy Warhol
Rorschach, 1984
Synthetic polymer paint on canvas
20 x 16 inches

Common Challenges of Small to Mid-size Visual Arts Spaces

The earliest and most comprehensive data on Initiative participants' fiscal and capacity circumstances came from the facilitated self-assessments. As was discussed earlier, these provided a full picture of each organization's individual situation; however, when looked at together, they also give a larger portrait of the kinds of issues that regularly confront these small contemporary arts groups. In general, the main problems the Initiative grantees struggle with are those the lifecycle model associates with organizations in the "growth stage": the moment at which programs have been successfully developed and have been recognized in the marketplace, but where management, governance, financial and internal capacities may lag behind.

This section describes the kinds of capacity challenges that most affected the initial thirty-one visual arts groups of the Initiative. Just as each participant used its lifecycle assessments to understand the specific challenges that confronted it, the foundation used its awareness of these broader issues to further develop and refine the Initiative's program design.

Mission and programming challenges. Despite the fact that many of these groups have two to three decades of programming experience and have presented hundreds if not thousands of artists over the course of their existences, at the program's outset, many Initiative participants described themselves as "unsuccessful" in articulating their organizations' and fields' rich histories and their valuable roles within the greater arts ecosystem. Although most had a passionate following among the artists they served most directly, many felt they lacked a clear, recognizable identity within the greater arts community, among wider arts audiences, donors and even other arts institutions. "Most critical to our success in the coming years will be our ability to communicate our relevance and importance to the public," wrote one participant; others noted that a key problem was a failure to consolidate the disparate attendees at various events into a consistent core audience with strong loyalty to the organization. Many participants had seen their audiences shift dramatically depending on the type of event they presented – small groups like these are flexible and may host different kinds of events ranging from exhibitions to films to poetry readings. In theory this range could be a strength, allowing the groups to reach and connect with a larger group of people; in practice, however, such diversity of programming can make it hard to establish a clear, memorable identity. Lack of funds and staff resources also limit these groups' ability to track audience data, which in turn makes marketing, audience development and fundraising efforts more difficult.

One Initiative grantee put her organization's challenge this way: "To stay true to our mission, we need to remain vital, current and relevant while expanding our future role in the local and national arts ecology." Yet limited financial resources make the kind of responsive programming envisioned here difficult for many. Likewise, the politically challenging nature of certain program content has occasionally had negative fundraising implications for the groups. Although as a general rule programming vision and execution are these organizations' greatest strengths, before the Initiative many had only limited experience with strategic or business planning. As a result they had a difficult time linking the value of their programming to any audience development or income generating efforts, or with setting goals or measuring accomplishments.

Management and staffing challenges. Staff recruitment was experienced as a struggle for all; below-market compensation and limited employee benefits compound difficulties in recruitment and retention. Although these dynamics tend to create flexible organizational structures, under-staffing is cited by most as the reason they lack depth in development, marketing, administrative, and technology positions. Burnout, along with having little money for self-renewal projects like professional development or networking with peers, represents another common manage-ment and staff challenge. Several organizations were concerned about founder/leadership succession planning. In the older, more established groups, said one participant, "Developing the next generation of leadership on both board and staff levels is a continual challenge."

Governance challenges. Many Initiative organizations have a core of dedicated supporters on their boards; boards also often have artists as members, who stand up for the artistic integrity of the organization and insist on the highest programming standards. These creative and committed board members are often one of an organization's greatest assets. However, the groups also badly need boards that can help them in some of their most challenging tasks: fundraising and networking within the community. They hope to build greater fiscal oversight and policy-making into their board structures and as a result need boards that have financial as well as cultural expertise. Most Initiative grantees are working hard to attract future board members with higher community profiles and financial resources; yet they feel at a disadvantage when pursuing them because they are not "major institutions." As one grantee put it, "Building our board of directors is our most critical challenge; that, and building an ever more diverse support base." As any good manager knows, accomplishing the first task will make the second easier; this is something the groups are working on.

Facilities challenges. As presenters of contemporary art, all these groups have unique space requirements. Whether it's square footage for gallery space, high ceilings, good natural light, or adequate storage, abundant and appropriate space is often critical to their work. At the start of the Initiative, a handful of groups owned their facilities or had some type of "in-kind" or concessionary lease that reduced or eliminated rent. But these were the exceptions. Most rented their spaces, and were thus extremely vulnerable to rising rents, displacement by developers, and neighborhood and building gentrification. At the time of the assessment, several groups either needed to relocate or were in the process of moving; many used Warhol funds to launch capital campaigns, undertake feasibility studies, or embark on the renovation of an old or development of a new space.

Financial challenges. The economic downturn, government cut-backs, and decreased foundation giving were consistent problems for all of the groups in the Initiative. Yet many showed great resourcefulness in response to their difficulties raising money, and had developed sources of earned income and built membership and individual donor bases. At the Initiative's outset, most had cash flow problems which they managed without access to a bank line of credit or internal cash reserves; and nearly all lacked access to long-term working capital. In the words of one grantee, "the constant challenge for all arts non-profits is to raise more funds to allow us to serve our mission. The ability to diversify our funding sources, and increase our individual support base is key."

Internal systems challenges. Before the Initiative, most participants had, understandably, invested as much as possible in programming and the staff that would deliver it. Unfortunately, however, given their scarcity of resources, this investment often occurred at the expense of "back room" systems and operational processes. Thus for most of the Initiative participants, infrastructure was chronically underfunded. Nearly all participants felt that they needed to upgrade their artmaking facilities by purchasing equipment and services for digital and other new media. Technology in general, and perhaps even more so that which is needed for administrative purposes like fundraising, marketing and archiving, was identified as a continual challenge. Some also were dissatisfied with their financial reporting systems, feeling they had outgrown their ability to adequately track financial data or anticipate financial problems.

The capacity needs collectively faced by these groups, although quite specific to the visual arts, fit squarely in the lifecycle model's growth stage, the stage where mission and programs have taken root in the marketplace, yet demand for service exceeds the organization's current structural and resource capacities. The capitalization model of capacity-building efforts is designed precisely to meet these kinds of challenges, and we found it effective at doing so, as the next section will show.

Measuring Impact

The Warhol Foundation launched its capacity-building Initiative with a very clear aim – to strengthen the organizational infrastructure and financial capacity of small and mid-size visual arts spaces, and by doing so to support and enhance their ongoing artist-centered work. The foundation invested a total of five million dollars over five years in the first phase of the Initiative. Nearly $4.2 million went directly to the thirty-one organizations. The bulk of these funds – nearly $3.6 million – was geared toward capitalization purposes (cash reserves, facility-related projects, and improved technological infrastructure) while participants spent the rest, about $630,000, for consultant-based technical assistance. The remaining $800,000 funded activities such as the facilitated self-assessment process, the two weekend retreats for executive directors and board chairs, program design and modification, annual evaluations, and program dissemination.

This section summarizes several key findings about the Initiative's impact on its first visual arts cohort. The questionnaires addressed program impact in three ways: first, through a set of rank-order questions administered to the executive directors and participating board members that were designed to measure perceived capacity changes; secondly, through solicitation and analysis of quantifiable data; and third, through a set of open-ended questions meant to capture participants' overall experience of the Initiative. The impact data contained in this chapter represent information gathered in the final (2004) evaluation from 94 percent (29 out of 31) of Initiative organizations. (Sabbaticals and illness prevented the participation of the two missing groups.) Throughout the section, the data are supplemented with participants' comments about their experiences during the program.

Perceived capacity change. The groups' executive directors unanimously agreed that the Initiative had substantially improved their organizations' ability to serve artists over the long-term. Since continued support for artists was a primary goal of the project, this was a very satisfactory outcome. "This is about the long-term, and strengthening our organizational structure and financial picture will help artists in the end" was one typical comment. More than 90 percent of participants also reported significant improvements in how management, board members and staff now view their organizations. "I can't tell you how reassuring it is and what a boost to our staff and board to know a national funder invested in our program out here in fly-over country. Sometimes we think we are out here all alone," said one director. Ninety percent also felt that the Initiative had enhanced public awareness of their organizations. Said one grantee, "In selecting us, the Initiative gave us an enhanced profile with other funders to attract more funds. It was a public recognition of our commitment to artists and the services we offer them."

Objective capacity change. Probably the most consistent and significant change in organizations' status from the beginning to the end of the program was their overall increase in net worth. Comparing 2004 financial data to the baseline information gathered at the program's outset, we found that 12 groups had cash reserves when they entered the program, and the average size of their beginning reserves was $58,940. At the Initiative's completion, 25 out of 29 groups reporting had established reserve funds, and the average reserve amount for all 25 was more than $90,000. The Initiative allowed the twelve groups with initial reserves to increase their cash holdings by 110 percent from $58,940 initially to an average of $123,828 in 2004. Of course, this is the direct result of the capitalization grants, but it still reflects an overall improvement in fiscal health – a defining feature of organizations with strong capacity. (It is important to note that those groups who received grants for cash reserves agreed to bring their reserve funds to full strength every 12 months.)

Endowments are another general measure of financial well-being for larger non-profits. At the beginning of the Initiative, six of the groups had endowments; their average value was $83,205. At the program's completion, one more had been added and the new average amount was well over $375,000. This growth suggests that the Warhol capitalization grants have given participants helpful leverage in their fundraising endeavours, and that groups have been able to use them as seed money to raise matching grants from other sources.

In addition, the number of groups owning their own space grew from five (Atlanta Contemporary, Intermedia Arts, Project Row Houses, Salina, SPACES) to seven (The Luggage Store, Out North). While ownership of one's own space certainly does not put an end to financial problems, it is an indicator of greater organizational stability, and represents another permanent asset on a group's balance sheet.

Perhaps the most significant, and encouraging, quantitative finding was that although the Initiative did not fund operating expenses, there was nonetheless a 36 percent increase in the median operating budgets for reporting organizations. In addition, their earned income as a percentage of other income increased from 17 percent in the baseline budgets to 25 percent in the 2004 results. We consider this upward trend toward earned income significant; it is yet another indication that organizations are making strategic financial choices, like revenue diversification, as part of their sustainable future.

Only two indicators remained flat or barely changed from the start of the program to its end. The average number of full-time staff employed by the 29 groups reporting increased by less than 10 percent, and the number of part-time staff (on average) decreased by about seven percent during the period. Perhaps some part-time staff moved to full-time positions; perhaps groups had already invested as much as they could in staffing before the program began. Given the chronic issues of staff overwork that plague these organizations, however, the continued low staffing levels (four or five people on average per group) do suggest that staffing remains a significant challenge despite the Initiative's efforts.

Participant benefit. In surveys on the program's effectiveness, both executive directors and board members felt that the Initiative's capitalization and technical assistance grants had had a powerful impact on their organizations. Executive directors especially noted that the impact of the cash reserves was psychological as well as financial. The knowledge that there was money in the bank gave staff members the peace of mind to begin thinking about the organization's long-term future, and how better administrative practices now could help bring about that future. This new confidence enabled important cultural changes within the organizations. As one director observed, "We have made great progress toward achieving our goals. Our progress as an organization goes beyond the actual funds received through the Initiative. Every step of our involvement in this program provided our organization's key staff and board members new opportunities for expanding their understanding."

The training that went along with the grants on how to use and account for the cash reserve awards, together with the freedom each group had in allocating the funds, helped to create a sense of fiduciary responsibility among both board members and management. "Although it always seems we are on the brink, the depth and reserve of knowledge and people has grown."

Program value. Participants were asked to rate the value and effectiveness of five specific program components: self-assessments; peer convenings; cash infusion grants; technical assistance; and program flexibility. All five of these components received "very valuable" marks by more than 90 percent of executive directors and board members. Said one, "It was a brilliant move ... The self-assessment had the biggest impact, it was critical to make us think about what we wanted to do and how we wanted to do it." The convenings too were greatly appreciated. "An incredible experience and of true value to us ... the support and shared ideas continue well after the retreat." Participants applauded the program's flexibility and were grateful for the way it offered them both guidance and the freedom to allocate their grant money: "The respect and flexibility given to organizations was critical. Also, the technical assistance added cohesion." When asked to list other valuable components of the Initiative, the most commonly cited items were access to consultants, philosophical support, recognition and credibility.

What issues remain as the Initiative's first phase comes to a close? Participants list four areas of continuing challenges, each involving a core capacity question that by its very nature may never be completely resolved. The first is the ongoing difficulty of recruiting and retaining strong, engaged board members who will be active in the organization, have a stake in its continued life and health, and, crucially, be able to either give or raise money. One participant sees such board members as key to her group's long-term vitality: "Our board has taken a positive turn but we need to keep the momentum going. This means seeking out qualified candidates and clarifying the role of existing members to increase active involvement. Together, these things will contribute to a self-perpetuating climate of investment in [the organization]." Although many feel the Initiative enhanced their board's functioning, recruitment remains a challenge for most.

A corresponding problem is the difficulty of recruiting and retaining high quality staff. The smaller organizations in particular cite inadequate salaries and benefits as among their chief recruitment and retention problems. Other organizations list burnout – a direct by-product, they feel, of insufficient staff capacity – as a major challenge. "Staff capacity to implement growth is still one of our most significant barriers to fully implement what we've learned in the Initiative."

The difficulty of raising money for contemporary visual art, particularly in a more conservative America, is a third concern. Participants know they need to build a more diverse support base to undergird their mission. Yet they are also realistic about ebbs and flows in donor support and are constantly working to develop additional earned revenue strategies. Some, particularly those in communities with high concentrations of arts organizations, face severe competition for dollars. The smaller groups view program and operating support as important elements of their financial future, while the larger ones emphasize the need to build long-term and committed relationships with foundations and individual donors who understand and support their mission. One participant voiced a universal sentiment: "Financial stability is the key."

Finally, the ability to find and afford adequate space was identified by most as a fourth challenge that will continue beyond the Initiative. Whether a group wishes to rent or to own, finding affordable space that is big enough and in the right location will not be easy. Maintaining adequate facilities reserves, especially for older buildings, is an expensive enterprise, and most groups cannot yet manage it. "Packaging facilities upgrades in a way that appeals to donors and other funders is a continual challenge." As space-based organizations, facilities will no doubt continue to be an ongoing challenge for all.

Lessons Learned

The Warhol Initiative's capacity-building work with its first set of participants began to wind down in December 2004. From this group of thirty-one visual arts organizations, the foundation learned several important lessons that will help inform the Initiative's next phase, set to begin in the spring of 2005. Here is a short list of these lessons; they may be of use to others considering similar projects.

Meeting them where they are. Understanding and valuing each participant's capacity starting point was an essential part of the Initiative's program design. And although the Initiative had a common set of program offerings, it was important to us, and to the grantees, that we perceive and treat each one as separate and unique. The lifecycle capacity framework adopted as the Initiative's organizing principle provided a theoretical and practical mechanism for tailoring both capitalization grants and technical assistance to each participant. Grantees found the model intuitive, non-judgmental, and a helpful tool for identifying "where they were" in relation to their own past achievements and future aims. The paradigm also seemed to encourage self-awareness in the participating organizations and to help them move forward more quickly in pursuit of their goals.

Achieving buy-in. The self-assessment had the beneficial effect of instilling a sense of ownership and responsibility for the organization's challenges in the staff and board members. Having themselves identified the key issues they faced, rather than having them pointed out by an outsider, they had a greater commitment to working towards change. Feedback on this feature was overwhelmingly positive, and while participants were aware that the lifecycle model was applied to all the groups, they found it flexible enough to incorporate their individual experiences, and did not feel oppressed by its imposition from outside.

Mission-related partnership. Creating a sense of partnership with grantees and treating them as colleagues with mutual interests also added to the Initiative's success. Many respondents commented that it was a new experience to feel like equal partners with a donor, instead of the more familiar experience of being subject to the foundation's rules and desires. Grantees felt that the peer convenings and their work with consultants and foundation staff created a sense of shared purpose among all the participants in the program.

Capacity-building in support of mission. From previous experiences the foundation had learned how easy it is to let capacity goals become ends rather than means. It therefore made sure that all the Initiative's capacity supports were clearly presented as being in the service of the mission and not ends in and of themselves. By and large, participants were able in this way to keep a fairly even balance in their focus on mission issues on the one hand and capacity issues on the other. In the peer programming, particularly the retreats, there was a strong emphasis on the importance of mission-capacity balance. Although board members in particular were eager for technical retreat topics (particularly around board development), the retreats were organized so that sharing innovative programming concepts and cutting edge work was a central part of the peer convenings.

Board ownership. It was a new experience for many board members to be involved in grant-related activities, and it proved to be very useful for many of them. From the very beginning, the Initiative required board participation in all its activities, from self-assessment to retreats; the foundation felt strongly that one of the keys to a strong and healthy organization is a sense of shared organizational ownership between staff leaders and the board. Achieving board buy-in and organizational ownership gave executive directors – who before the program were often the only ones with a strong understanding of their organizations' operational side –

new partners who were aware of their shared responsibility for the group's future. Indeed, involving board members in the self-assessment, retreats, and other activities may prove to be one of the most durable and change-producing of the Initiative's activities.

Cash reserves – a bridge toward the future. There is no doubt that the $125,000 capitalization grants were a significant inducement for Initiative participants to apply to the program and then to work to improve their organization's management. But the most important thing about these grants turned out to be structuring them as working capital. Traditionally, philanthropy has had two means of providing financial capacity assistance to organizations: endowment funds for long-term aid, and operating support for the immediate term. While these methods both help groups to meet certain goals, neither provides the dynamic type of future-oriented capital small and mid-size organizations need most. Cash reserves gave Warhol participants two important gifts: the reality of a more financially secure future and the confidence and ability to plan ahead that goes with it.

Perceived flexibility. The program's flexibility was a surprisingly important benefit. Although all the organizations received similar grants, they chose many different ways to make use of them. While some used the full grant amount to establish a cash reserve, others used some of the money to pay down a mortgage, allocating the rest to reserves. Others bought computer equipment or were finally able to move to a new location. The freedom to use the money as the staff and board leaders saw best also encouraged reflection and a sense of responsibility in the participants as they considered what the best strategic use of this "windfall" might be. Many groups had never before had the opportunity to make such financially significant decisions, and most felt they had learned a lot in the process.

Small things convey respect. Perhaps the most consistent comment from Initiative participants, one which reappeared in every annual evaluation of the program, was that the program showed a strong sensitivity to and respect for its grantees. Often the things that most strongly conveyed that respect – the application stipend, the self-assessment process, the willingness to let grantees decide how to use their Initiative funds – were components that cost the foundation little or nothing and were relatively easy to provide. They had the effect, though, of nurturing grantees' trust in the foundation, and as a result, there was little conflict between donor and recipient over the course of the project.

Process drives outcomes. Thus, we believe that the program's positive outcomes were due as much to the way it was constructed as to the quantity of funding and technical assistance it offered. From the outset, we set out to engage each organization at several levels; to provide flexibility for each to understand and prioritize its own needs; and at the same time to convey the foundation's deep respect for the visual arts field, and for each organization's own work.

Work has begun on a second phase of the Warhol Initiative – a three-year, $3 million program intended to benefit the next generation of contemporary visual arts spaces. While the participants in the first phase were organizations that had been founded during the 1970s and '80s, those in the second phase were mostly founded after 1995. These groups tend to have smaller budgets than their predecessors; most are under $300,000. Younger as organizations, they also tend to have younger leaders; most of the directors founded their groups and are still in their twenties and thirties. While their basic missions – to serve artists and show innovative contemporary work – are indistinguishable from those of the Initiative's first cohort, these second-phase organizations often have different visions of how to achieve their artistic and organizational goals. Many of the directors have already worked as curators or administrators at contemporary arts organizations and have adopted different management structures than their older counterparts.

Andy Warhol
<u>Vote McGovern</u>, 1972
Screenprint on Arches paper
42 x 42 inches

Grants for the Initiative's second-phase groups will be made for the same essential purpose: to strengthen their continued capacity to deliver vibrant, relevant programming in service to artists. But since the majority of these groups are at an earlier stage of lifecycle development – most in the start-up, as opposed to the growth stage – their capacity work will be focused differently. The aim with these groups is to help them get safely through their initial developmental stages so that they can build enduring organizations. They need to establish themselves and make their product and their services better known in the marketplace. It is our hope that the Initiative's guidance will make it easier for them to put professional management practices in place from the beginning, so that infrastructure issues will not hold them back as they grow. Grant awards for this group aim to help them develop sound managerial and board practices and to design and realize a sustainable, long-term artistic identity.

The application process for the Initiative's second phase began in late fall 2004, with selection in early 2005. To learn more about these groups' shared characteristics, strengths and challenges, the foundation convened a focus group of prototypical smaller visual arts groups. Our observations, which we will use to help design the second phase's programming, follow.

Practical and realistic. As a whole, these groups have a very practical and realistic attitude towards the management of their organizations, and start from the assumption that strong management and financial structures are essential to their ability to serve artists. They are aware of the difficulties inherent in presenting progressive art in today's political environment, and have shown themselves to be politically adept both in fundraising and in attracting audiences. They are focused on making development systems work for them and are good at looking for funding where it is available.

Interest in organizational matters. These groups also show a keen interest in accountability and compliance matters, particularly with regard to the implications of their tax-exempt status. They know how important it is to understand the limitations that tax exemption puts on their activities, but also want to know about different business and funding models that could be useful for them. While they recognize the importance of foundations as a source of funding, they know they must also pursue strategies for earning income, cultivating individual donors, and for accessing "non-arts-specific" government funding such as that available for neighborhood organizations.

Alternative space validation. In the focus group, the directors of these smaller organizations made clear that they see their spaces as an alternative to larger or more mainstream organizations. They adamantly rejected the notion that their organizations are mere junior versions of these groups, stepping stones for either administrators or artists with higher ambitions. Instead, these directors feel that their mandate is to create more professional options for artists, administrators and curators, who can now choose to work primarily in these alternative spaces, move from them to mainstream organizations, or go back and forth between the two. For these young arts professionals, a successful career no longer must follow a one-way path from small and obscure venues to larger, more prominent ones. Instead, they see a much wider arts landscape, in which arts professionals can choose amongst a variety of spaces according to their interests, desires, or the exigencies of a given moment in their careers. In this vision of the art world, small alternative spaces are vital sources of artist support and offer some of many important exhibition opportunities. The leaders of these groups also feel strongly that it is their role to provide validation to local and regional artists, and to show that it is not necessary for them to move to New York or Los Angeles to prove their professional legitimacy or have successful careers.

Emerging and mid-career artists. These groups see themselves as serving both emerging and mid-career artists. The directors spoke passionately about discovering and presenting emerging artists, but also felt they had much to offer to more established ones who might wish to take their work in a new direction, present riskier material, or who are having difficulties finding venues because they are no longer the "hot new thing." Of course, these are all roles played by the organizations in the Initiative's first phase, but it was good to hear these younger groups express the same strong commitment to serving artists that their more established peers have.

Invigorated by peer interaction. Like the Initiative's first groups, these directors were very interested in and invigorated by peer interaction, and they freely exchanged ideas and practices. They seemed to be lacking a strong proprietary relation to the information and strategies they had developed; perhaps they had been influenced by an Internet culture that takes for granted the importance of the free exchange of information. Perhaps also they have more of a sense of how important it is for all the groups' survival in a challenging climate to have a strong sense of community and shared purpose.

Founding role. One of the key challenges for the first group of Initiative participants was the question of succession: how does a founding director manage to disengage from the organization he or she created when the time comes, and how can leadership structures be put in place beforehand to ease that transition? This second group seemed already to be aware of this as a potential issue in their futures. Most of the focus group participants were founders, but they already realized the importance of keeping their own identities separate from those of their organizations. Many founders in this group talked specifically about the importance of allowing the founder's role to change as the organization grows; they also recognized that the real test of this will come when the organization, whether because of the influence of board members, staff, or artists, starts to head in a direction that the founder has not chosen.

Self-defined success. These directors believe it is important for them to proactively define and articulate measurable indices of success for their type of organization. They do not wish to be seen as "mini" versions of older or larger spaces, and feel they must develop a set of benchmarks for themselves that will accurately reflect their own organizational goals and ambitions.

The following organizations have been accepted for the second phase of the Warhol Initiative, and the foundation is in the process of designing a program that will address their particular needs and desires. As in the Initiative's first phase, monetary grants, technical assistance and peer programming will be the core components, but as the foundation learns more about the Phase Two groups, it will tailor the project's execution to their particular capacity issues.

Warhol Initiative Participants. Phase Two

Artspace New Haven

Aurora Picture Show Houston

Franklin Art Works Minneapolis

Locust Projects Miami

Midway Contemporary Art Minneapolis

Momenta Art Brooklyn

PARTICIPANT INC New York

Ruby Green Contemporary Art Center Nashville

Smack Mellon Studios Brooklyn

The Soap Factory Minneapolis

TRANS > New York

Transformer Incorporated Washington, D.C.

Andy Warhol
Crowd, c. 1963
Graphite and screenprint
on Strathmore paper
28½ x 22⅝ inches

The Warhol Initiative has been an ambitious attempt to improve the financial and operating capacity of an important set of contemporary visual arts spaces, a constituency that has historically been both underfunded and without the consistent support of a national service organization. That the first phase of the Initiative took place between 1999 and 2005, a period that witnessed the September eleventh terrorist attacks on New York City, the subsequent downturn in the stock market, and a national decline and retrenchment in arts giving, gives further weight to the program's universally positive reception, critical impact and positive results.

Andy Warhol
One Dollar Bills, 1962
Screenprint on rice paper
34 x 24¾ inches

At five million dollars over five years, the Initiative has not been, financially speaking, a large venture. But its impact has been immense. Participants have credited the Initiative with, among other things, increasing their capacity to present high-quality exhibitions and performances; expanding their programs for the professional education of artists; improving their facilities so they could attract their "highest gallery attendance ever"; and getting artists more integrally involved in planning and growth efforts. Each of these achievements has a direct relation to better programming for artists, even though the Initiative's specific supports were financially and operationally focused. As one pleased participant said, "The Warhol Initiative has opened the gates for us. We are able to move forward to sustainability and create an exciting new arena with our artists' initiatives."

The Warhol Initiative served thirty-one contemporary art spaces in its first phase, and will soon begin work with a second set of twelve smaller groups that also provide progressive, front-line services to visual artists in their communities. As with the first, the Initiative's second phase will deliver financial support and technical resources designed around the specific needs of these grantees. It will use a lifecycle assessment framework and build in the flexibility and respectful delivery that the first group saw as so important to the program's success.

Unless giving trends substantially improve, raising money will continue to be a challenge for the visual arts. We hope this report will encourage other foundations and individuals interested in contemporary art to increase their programmatic and capital funding to the small and mid-size visual arts organizations that are so important to the ecology and careers of emerging and mid-career artists. With their financial and operating capacity significantly strengthened through the Initiative, these contemporary art spaces are now better candidates for investment than they were before. Indeed, with the Initiative's support, these groups have, as they put it, "put long range plans into effect"; "have a much clearer sense of our financial standing at any given time"; "have attracted higher level board candidates"; and "are moving ... governance responsibilities to higher levels." These testimonials speak to these groups' increased strategic, financial, governance and management capacity – which, along with their enhanced ability to serve artists, was the Initiative's entire purpose in launching a capacity-building project.

We end this report confident that the Warhol Initiative, in addition to strengthening the groups' financial and operating structures, has reinforced both the self-awareness and the adaptability of the boards and management of thirty-one contemporary art spaces. As of this writing, twelve more are about to begin the process, and all will continue to provide on-the-ground support to artists, the heart of our creative society.

For additional copies of this report, or to learn more about the Initiative, please contact The Andy Warhol Foundation info@warholfoundation.org, or Susan Kenny Stevens at psg@larsonallen.com.

Andy Warhol
Daily News, 1967
Screenprint on paper
50 x 30 inches

Warhol Initiative Phase One.

Aljira, a Center for Contemporary Art. Newark, NJ
Aljira was created in 1983 in a third floor walk-up in downtown Newark. Its founders chose the name "aljira"– an Australian Aboriginal word meaning "dreamtime"– to signify their desire to create a space and sense of possibility for the "other" in society. From their first experimental exhibition until now, Aljira has received continued critical acclaim for its exhibitions and programs. Aljira's community role has also expanded to include graphic design services, professional development advice for emerging artists, an annual art auction showcasing more than 80 contemporary artists, and innovative arts education projects in local community schools.

Art in General. New York, NY
Located in lower Manhattan, Art in General was founded in 1981 by a group of artists in search of a space to exhibit their work. Today, Art in General is a laboratory for new art, and has presented more than 4,000 emerging and underrepresented artists in visual arts, photography, video, audio, performance and new media over the past twenty-four years. Annual visitors for its public programs exceed 26,000; a website and publications extend the organization's programs beyond the exhibition space.

Artists Space. New York, NY
Founded in 1972, Artists Space provides an exhibition space for new art and artists, encourages experimentation, diversity and dialogue in contemporary arts practice, and fosters an appreciation for the vital role that artists play in our community. Artists Space offers opportunities for artists at a critical juncture in their careers, including exhibitions, an emerging curators series, project grants, Survival Skills workshops, and the Irving Sandler Artists File, a digital image database and slide registry that

is accessible to the public at the gallery and online. Over the years, Artists Space has introduced over 6,000 emerging artists, many of whom are now at the top of the profession.

Atlanta Contemporary Art Center. Atlanta, GA
Founded in 1973, Atlanta Contemporary Art Center (known locally as "the Contemporary") is a multidisciplinary arts center that contributes to Atlanta's arts scene by presenting the work of local, regional, national, and international artists to the Greater Atlanta community. Programming reflects the Contemporary's dedication to both experimentation and artistic excellence in contemporary art; arts education is also a major priority. It presents gallery exhibitions, has an education and outreach program, and houses twelve studio workspaces.

Center for Women & Their Work. Austin, TX
Founded by three women artists at the height of the artists space and women's movement in 1978, the Center for Women & Their Work is a multidisciplinary art organization that presents fifty events a year and has exhibited over 1,700 artists since its founding. Dedicated to furthering the public's understanding of the work it presents and of contemporary art in general, it produces color brochures on each exhibition with interpretive essays on the artists. It also has a comprehensive education program for children that serves over 2,500 students and teachers annually.

CEPA Gallery. Buffalo, NY
Founded in 1974, CEPA Gallery is an arts center dedicated to the creation and presentation of photo-related and digital art, and to educating the public about this important field. The gallery presents work and supports projects by both established and emerging visual artists

from across the country, and is committed to supporting artists from groups that have been traditionally underrepresented in cultural spaces. In addition to the gallery, CEPA curates several public art sites around the city of Buffalo. On an annual basis CEPA serves several hundred artists, over 1,000 urban youth, and over 250,000 visitors and viewers of its public art program.

Creative Time. New York, NY

Founded in 1972, Creative Time has commissioned, produced, and presented adventurous temporary public artworks by thousands of artists of all disciplines. It specializes in projects that free artists from the limitations of traditional gallery spaces, and collaborates with them to realize innovative new works that expand their practice while offering millions of people inspiring and engaging encounters with art.

Dieu Donné Papermill. New York, NY

Dieu Donné's roots date back more than 25 years to 1976. Originally an actual papermill, Dieu Donné has since become a space for artists to explore the potential of paper as an integrated art form, not merely a surface medium. Today, Dieu Donné is an artist workspace dedicated to the creation and promotion of contemporary art using the hand-papermaking process. Programs include artist residencies for emerging and mid-career artists, an educational outreach program, artist services for custom projects, and a gallery. Over the years, Dieu Donné has served over 500 artists and 2,500 papermaking students.

DiverseWorks. Houston, TX

DiverseWorks was founded in 1982 to provide a non-commercial space for artists in the Houston area. Since that time, DiverseWorks has broadened its programming to include national artists in the visual, performing and literary arts. It provides first-time commissioning opportunities for emerging artists and acts as a catalyst for new work by young artists and arts organizations. DiverseWorks now serves over 300 artists and 20,000 visitors per year.

Exit Art. New York, NY

Exit Art was founded in 1982 by a curator and an artist as an alternative to the commercial galleries and large cultural institutions in New York. Exit Art's multidisciplinary exhibitions and programs express a unique creative vision that frequently challenges traditional notions of what art is and offers new opportunities to bring together the artist and the public. It has earned renown for its curatorial innovation, programming in diverse media, and especially for discovering and showing the work of important but underrecognized artists.

509 Cultural Center aka The Luggage Store. San Francisco, CA

Since 1987, 509 Cultural Center/The Luggage Store Project Space has served as a link between artists, the local communities of the South of Market and Tenderloin districts, and the broader San Francisco art world. It provides a venue for multidisciplinary exhibitions and performances, community forums, arts education programs, and public arts projects and also hosts the annual In the Street Theater Festival.

Galería de la Raza. San Francisco, CA

Founded in 1970, Galería's programs explore contemporary issues in Latino art, culture and civic society. Galería serves Latino artists working in literary, performance, and visual art through exhibitions and multidisciplinary public events. It also has several educational and professional programs for artists: ReGeneration, a mentorship program for emerging artists; the Digital Mural Program, a new public art project on its Bryant Street billboard; Youth & Public Media, a training program for youth of color in digital media; and a gift shop selling artists' work, Studio 24.

Hallwalls Contemporary Arts Center. Buffalo, NY

Hallwalls was founded in 1974 by a group of young visual artists and art students seeking opportunities to promote their work and that of other emerging artists. Over the course of its thirty year history, Hallwalls has successfully supported thousands of artists in a wide range of mediums, many of whom have gone on to become major figures in their fields. Today Hallwalls draws up to 20,000 people a year to its programs in the visual arts, film, video, jazz and new music, and also hosts artist residencies, performances, and literary readings.

Headlands Center for the Arts. Sausalito, CA

Founded in 1982, Headlands Center for the Arts is a laboratory for creativity where artists experiment, collaborate and develop new work in a breathtaking coastal wilderness location near San Francisco. Headlands offers extended live-in and live-out residencies to as many as 30 artists from throughout the U.S. and the world each year; it also rents studio space to local artists. Through residencies and public programs, Headlands seeks to explore and interpret the relationship between place and the creative process, and to increase contemporary society's recognition of and appreciation for artists.

Intermedia Arts. Minneapolis, MN

Founded in 1973 to explore social issues through the then-new technology of video, Intermedia Arts has since become a multidisciplinary center dedicated to building understanding through art. Its programs try to create a context in which differing perspectives on social, political, and artistic issues can be presented and discussed openly. Intermedia Arts has been nationally recognized for its presentation of new art forms, its successful education and leadership programs, unique services to artists, and multidisciplinary public exhibitions and performances. The organization has up to 45,000 visitors per year, and serves over 700 artists.

Kansas City Artists Coalition. Kansas City, MO

The Kansas City Artists Coalition (KCAC) was founded in 1975 by a small group of artists interested in supporting their peers and increasing the knowledge and appreciation of contemporary art in the community. KCAC has presented over 200 exhibitions which have included approximately 3,500 artists in solo, two-person and group exhibitions; attendance is estimated at a quarter of a million. KCAC also publishes books, catalogs and directories of artists' work, funds international research for visual artists, and provides educational programs for artists and the community. KCAC has a membership of 1,000 artists and patrons.

Legion Arts. Cedar Rapids, IA

Incorporated in 1981 in New York City, Legion Arts moved to Cedar Rapids in 1994, where it now presents regional and national multidisciplinary contemporary artists in an historic building and other community locations. Legion Arts supports young artists in experimental arts forms, and works to involve artists and the arts in community development and neighborhood building.

Los Angeles Contemporary Exhibitions. Los Angeles, CA

Los Angeles Contemporary Exhibitions (LACE) originated in 1978 from a need for a Los Angeles venue that supports, exhibits, and advocates innovations in art-making. Since its inception, the organization has presented the work of 5,000 artists in 3,000 exhibitions, performances, screenings, and works of public art. LACE attracts visitors and tourists of diverse ages, income levels and cultural backgrounds, and exposes a broad community to art that other organizations may be reluctant to present.

MACLA/Movimiento de Arte y Cultura Latino Americana. San Jose, CA

MACLA, which stands for Movimiento de Arte y Cultura Latino Americana, began in 1989 as a grassroots community advocacy organization aimed at mobilizing multicultural city arts support. Since that time, MACLA has attracted local and national funding and has emerged as a contemporary arts space that showcases work by and about the Latino community. In addition to visual, literary, and performing arts programming, MACLA is also active in youth arts education.

New Langton Arts. San Francisco, CA

Founded in 1975 as an artists' collective for experimental visual and performing arts, Langton operates a gallery and theater and also has an online program. In these venues, it presents local, national and international artists working in the fields of visual art, literature, music, performance art, and net and video art. Langton attracts over 16,000 visitors a year, and is a known and valued source for new art and art forms; Langton's programming is also enhanced by the organization's commitment to providing documentation and other educational resources alongside its exhibits and programs.

911 Media Arts. Seattle, WA

911 Media Arts was founded in 1981 to create a space showcasing independent film, video, and multimedia arts and to provide media artists with access to exhibition space and other resources. Since that time, 911 Media Arts has promoted the use of innovative media through a variety of programs including workshops, screenings, rental production facilities and equipment, residencies, gallery exhibitions, and special programming for youth. Through its diverse programming, 911 Media Arts serves over 18,000 people per year.

Out North. Anchorage, AK

Out North was founded by artists and activists who wanted to challenge and inspire their local community through art and the creation of an innovative public forum for viewing and discussing it. Incorporated in 1985, Out North continues to make challenging contemporary art happen, earning grants from national organizations and wide press coverage for its mix of public art, youth arts education, and artist residencies and commissions, while remaining committed to its core values of supporting artistic creation, freedom of expression, and social change.

Project Row Houses. Houston, TX

Project Row Houses was founded in 1993, in twenty-two abandoned shotgun houses in Houston's historic Third Ward. Its aim was to create community through the celebration of art and African American history and culture. Since then, Project Row Houses has expanded its vision of art-making to include historic preservation, community development, education and social services programming. The Project Row House site now contains thirty-nine buildings that house its various projects: art, photography, and literary work; transitional housing for young mothers and their children; a gift shop; the Historic El Dorado ballroom; two parks; and a community garden.

Real Art Ways. Hartford, CT

Real Art Ways was founded in 1975 by a group of artists who created a live/work space in a loft in downtown Hartford. In 1990, Real Art Ways moved into an old typewriter factory, and in 1994 it began to develop 13,000 square feet of unfinished space in that building. Now its space houses a cinema, four gallery spaces, and the Loading Dock Lounge for socializing, and Real Art Ways continues its commitment to artists and its community with these expanded resources. The organization has developed a large local audience and membership base, and more than 40,000 people a year visit its cinema, exhibitions, concerts, performance, and spoken word events. It has over a thousand members.

Salina Art Center. Salina, KS

Founded in 1978, the Salina Art Center is committed to the visual arts, artists, and audiences in Salina and across the region. The Salina Art Center has been recognized for its innovative and vibrant exhibitions and programs, including the permanent Interactive Area for children of all ages. Its Art Center Cinema presents the best in contemporary American and international film. More than 40,000 children and adults across the state of Kansas participate in Salina Art Center events and programs each year.

San Francisco Camerawork. San Francisco, CA

Founded in 1974, SF Camerawork encourages emerging and mid-career artists to explore new directions in photography and related media by fostering creative forms of expression that push existing boundaries. Through exhibitions, publications, and educational programs, SF Camerawork stimulates public dialogue and inquiry about contemporary image-making in the context of current social and aesthetic issues. With an annual audience of more than 20,000 people, SF Camerawork is nationally recognized for its innovative programming and has been a launching pad for many successful artists' careers.

Self-Help Graphics. Los Angeles, CA

Self-Help Graphics was formed in 1971 as a place to create art that reflects the values and spirit of the local Chicano community. Today, Self-Help Graphics continues to serve local artists, as well as artists throughout the United States, Mexico and Latin America, and introduces audiences from around the world to Chicano arts, artists and culture. Current artistic programming includes a printmaking atelier, an exhibition print program and professional artists' workshops. Its youth arts programming and an onsite gallery, Galeria Otra Vez, enhance Self-Help Graphics' status as a vital arts resource for East Los Angeles.

Southern Exposure. San Francisco, CA

Southern Exposure has been presenting dynamic cutting edge art and community programs since 1974. An artist-run organization, Southern Exposure reaches out to diverse audiences and serves as a forum and resource center that supports the Bay Area's arts and education communities. Programs include visual arts exhibitions of new and risk-taking work by emerging artists, other public programming events, and the *Artists in Education Program* (AIE), which presents innovative artistic and cultural material to hundreds of high school students annually.

Space One Eleven. Birmingham, AL

The name Space One Eleven refers to the Birmingham street address where the organization was founded in 1986. From the outset, Space One Eleven offered area artists a venue for their work and the opportunity to connect with other artists. With its move to its current site near a large public housing complex, it expanded its programming to deal with the kinds of social, economic and political issues that affect both contemporary art and the community. Today, Space One Eleven provides professional opportunities for artists, creates a forum for increased public understanding of contemporary art, and offers arts education to area youth.

SPACES. Cleveland, OH

Founded in 1978 by artists, SPACES is the most visible artist-run organization in Ohio dedicated to supporting alternative art. In pursuit of its mandate to advance the artist's vision, SPACES supports the creation of new work by contemporary area, national and international artists, bringing them to Cleveland to engage the public in vital dialogues about contemporary art. It works to foster real communication between artists and the community through public programs, informal opportunities for exchange, national and international artists' residencies, and publications. A diverse annual audience of 15,000 includes artists of all ages and disciplines, students from kindergarten through college, families, professionals, and various ethnic communities.

White Columns. New York, NY

Founded in 1969, White Columns is New York City's oldest alternative art space. From the beginning, White Columns' mission has been to give voice to artists early in their career. Hundreds of young artists have gotten their start through the ongoing exhibition program which presents new work in all media to New York audiences. White Columns exhibits nearly 200 emerging artists each year and draws 1,200 visitors monthly.

Warhol Initiative Phase Two.

Artspace. New Haven, CT

Founded in 1984, Artspace is an artist-run contemporary arts organization in New Haven whose mission is to foster new work by artists, providing them with a range of opportunities to engage audiences. Its core programs are the untitled (space) gallery, a lab for emerging curators featuring bi-monthly exhibitions in all media; the Flatfile, a permanent archive containing works on paper by 100 promising artists from the region; the Lot, a public art space on an open parcel of land just off the New Haven Green; and City-Wide Open Studios, an annual event in which 400 artists participate, and which draws 15,000 visitors from across the region.

Aurora Picture Show. Houston, TX

Aurora Picture Show is a film and media center founded in 1998 by two artists in Houston. It presents independent and experimental works and supports artists through exhibition opportunities and the promotion of their work, as well as through artist fees (more than $25,000 annually). Housed in a converted church building, Aurora is the only venue of its kind in the Southwest; its human scale and focus on community help it to promote fertile exchanges between artists and audiences.

Franklin Art Works. Minneapolis, MN

Franklin Art Works is a visual and performing arts center established in 1999 and located in a renovated silent-era movie theater. It is dedicated to presenting cutting-edge contemporary work by local and national artists. Through a mix of exhibitions, performing arts, film and arts education, Franklin Art Works celebrates contemporary art in all its complexity and diversity. With its ongoing development of the arts center, the organization aims to become both a locus of artistic innovation and a center for social interaction and engagement with art.

Locust Projects. Miami, FL

Locust Projects is located in an industrial building in the warehouse district of Miami. It produces and presents contemporary installations in various media, including video and performance art. Locust Projects was founded by artists in 1998 in response to the growing need for exhibition opportunities for area artists and with a focus on providing them with a forum to experiment and test new ideas.

Midway Contemporary Art. Minneapolis, MN

Founded in 2000, Midway Contemporary Art is a gallery committed to encouraging innovation and diversity in the visual arts. It offers emerging and underrepresented artists from the region and abroad a public platform for presenting their work, supports significant new developments in the field, and works to stimulate and nurture an ongoing public discussion of contemporary art and culture.

Momenta Art. Brooklyn, NY

Originally established in Philadelphia in 1986, Momenta Art is an exhibition space now located in Williamsburg, Brooklyn. Its mission is to promote the work of emerging artists through two-person shows in which the artists have the opportunity to present substantial bodies of work in separate project spaces. For most of these artists it is their first opportunity to exhibit in New York City.

PARTICIPANT INC. New York, NY

Founded in 2002, PARTICIPANT, Inc. is located in a storefront on the Lower East Side of New York City. With an emphasis on artist-driven curatorial practice, it is a venue that promotes artistic experimentation, exploration, and solo interdisciplinary projects. Working with artists, curators, writers, and educators, PARTICIPANT develops programs that combine various mediums and encourage the intersection of the visual, media, literary, and performing arts. The organization makes contemporary art accessible to the public through interactive exhibitions, as well as screenings, performances, and educational programs.

Ruby Green Contemporary Art Center. Nashville, TN

Ruby Green Contemporary Art Center is dedicated to the promotion of contemporary and progressive art by emerging and established artists, and to furthering the creative exchange of ideas through exhibits, events and programs. Since its founding in 1998, Ruby Green has provided both exhibition space and critical forums for emerging and established artists, and has focused particularly on those whose work takes an interdisciplinary approach and/or has strong conceptual elements.

Smack Mellon Studios. Brooklyn, NY

Originating in 1995 by a sculptor and a musician as a series of informal artist get-togethers, Smack Mellon is now an arts organization located in the DUMBO area of Brooklyn. Smack Mellon assists artists in the creation and exhibition of new work by providing exhibition opportunities, studio workspace, and access to equipment and the technical assistance that can enable ambitious projects that might not otherwise be possible. The organization's new location in a large industrial building on the waterfront will offer expansive facilities for the exhibition and artist residency program.

The Soap Factory. Minneapolis, MN
The Soap Factory is a visual arts organization dedicated
to supporting emerging artists, enhancing the public's
understanding and appreciation of their work, and
fostering strength and vitality in the arts, cultural, and
educational communities of the Twin Cities. Founded
in 1988 by local artists, it was one of the first organizations
in the area to regularly provide a venue exclusively
devoted to new and emerging visual artists. In recent
years, the organization has relocated to a former soap
factory, a turn-of-the-century wood and brick warehouse
that provides a raw industrial space and unique showcase for all types of media.

TRANS>. New York, NY
TRANS> is an arts and culture organization dedicated
to the support of innovative contemporary artists and the
critical contextualization of their work. Presenting artist
projects in the U.S. and abroad, it opened an exhibition
space in the Chelsea neighborhood in 2002. TRANS>
also has a publishing division, which produces an art
journal, books and monographs. The organization's
overall mission is to bring cutting edge art and cultural
production to an international public.

Transformer Incorporated. Washington, D.C.
Transformer is an artist-centered arts organization
founded in 2002 that connects and promotes emerging
artists locally, nationally and internationally. Partnering
with artists, curators, art spaces and other cultural
entities, Transformer serves as a catalyst and advocate
for emergent expression in the visual arts.

Aljira, a Center for Contemporary Art
591 Broad Street
Newark, New Jersey 07102
973 622 1600
973 622 6526 fax
aljira.org

Aljira's staff in the main gallery. Eathon Hall, Matt Brown, Sam Larson, Lisa R. Saroop, Amanda Cachia, Victor L. Davson, Cicely Cottingham, and Bambang Widodo.

Moved by Awe. An exhibition featuring the work of the eighteen participating artists from the *Aljira Emerge 2001* professional development program.

lling the following objectives:
or artists working outside of
lidating art of diverse cultural
ituates work exhibited in
ationship to the mainstream;
cultural, racial and social
m of cultural presentations;
ating on community-based
d being a focal point and home
that weave together the arts,
 education.

Aljira achieves its mission by
creating exhibition opportunit
the commercial gallery system
origins; providing a context th
a dialectical or an educationa
responding to America's dram
changes through a broad spe
creating, supporting, and collc
programming related to the art
base for grassroots organizati
neighborhoods, and institutior

Beginning with the search by a group of young artists for affordable workspace in Newark, Aljira was officially founded as an exhibition space in 1984 by artists Victor L. Davson and Carl E. Hazlewood. By choosing Aljira as its name, a word from the Australian Aborigines which means "dreamtime," the founders signaled their desire to create a space and a sense of possibility for the art of the "other," that is, for artists outside the mainstream.

The Warhol Initiative leveraged the support of key community stakeholders, a requirement necessary to fund, sustain and build stable systems in support of art programs such as Aljira's. Specifically, it facilitated Aljira's move to its new 6,000-square-foot facility in the heart of Newark's downtown business and cultural district, making its exhibitions, education and public programs accessible to the broadest audiences possible. These programs and the new location have garnered significant media attention from national newspapers and major trade journals.

fit organization located
rovides a laboratory
st of today's art–work
ted in art museums
With exhibitions drawn
artists' projects created
r of public programs,
ved into a magnet and
sted in new ways of
ary art.

Art in General's staff members and interns participate in
New Zealand artist Ani O'Neill's interactive residency project
entitled *The Buddy System*. Visitors learned how to crochet

View from the corner of Walker Street and Cortland Alley.
Art in General's entrance and ground-level Project Space with a
commissioned, site-specific installation by Jaime Ruiz Otis, 2004.

Art in General
79 Walker Street
New York, New York 10013
212 219 0473
212 219 0511 fax
artingeneral.org

Artists Space was founded in 1972 by Trudie Grace and Irving Sandler with a $100,000 grant from the New York State Council on the Arts (NYSCA). The Committee for the Visual Arts was incorporated as a service and arts organization in 1972, and its gallery, Artists Space, opened its first season in October 1973 at 155 Wooster Street.

The Warhol Initiative considerably impacted Artists Space on several levels. The technology grant allowed us to upgrade and streamline office infrastructure, and in particular assisted in the expansion of the capabilities of the Artists File and the launch of the *Artists File Online* which has also resulted in a stronger international web presence.

Warhol support also helped us leverage increased funding from other sources. Since the receipt of Warhol Initiative funds, we have doubled artistic program budgets while increasing administrative costs by just 10%.

One of New York's
galleries boasting
internationally rec[o]
artists, Artists Spa[c]
provides services [
at a critical junctu[r]
promoting experim[
within contempor[a]

st non-profit art
n alumni roster of
nized contemporary
exhibits and
emerging artists
in their careers,
tation and diversity
arts practice.

Establishing Shot. Exhibition featuring work by Gareth James. Entitled: "S" is for Storm, or how a sketch of a building housing an artist's studio seen from a great height could be misrepresented, almost as though something which – as yet – had little by way of what could be called reality or realty about itself, desired a pseudonym, a way of holding off its encroaching actualization and diminishing potentiality, or, how the artist Billy Nomates taught us finally how to live without an audience along the way to elaborating an

The view from our window. Artists Space.

Artists Space
38 Greene Street
New York, New York 10013
212 226 3970
212 966 1434 fax
artistsspace.org

The Contemporary was founded in 1973 as a storefront cooperative gallery by a group of Atlanta photographers who sought freedom to experiment and to exhibit their work on their own terms. The gallery, supported by member dues and staffed by volunteers, staged monthly exhibits of local, regional and national photographers.

Since announcement of the Warhol Initiative grant to the Contemporary in the spring of 2003, we have eliminated our debt, reduced our annual operating budget to bring expenses in line with realistic income expectations, put in place an internal operating cash reserve of $90,000, and completely replaced and upgraded our computer technology and systems.

The Contemporary was founded in 1973 as a storefront cooperative gallery by a group of Atlanta photographers who sought freedom to experiment and to exhibit their work on their own terms. The gallery, supported by member dues and staffed by volunteers, staged monthly exhibits of local, regional and national photographers.

Since announcement of the Warhol Initiative grant to the Contemporary in the spring of 2003, we have eliminated our debt, reduced our annual operating budget to bring expenses in line with realistic income expectations, put in place an internal operating cash reserve of $90,000, and completely replaced and upgraded our computer technology and systems.

The Atlanta Contemporary Art Cen
experimentation and education in
provide access to resources and s
artists on local, regional, national
opportunities for them to share the
of its programming, The Contempo
and cultural diversity. By develop
energetic audiences of knowledge
multidisciplinary arts center in the

During the summer of 2004, IMAGI
the 535 Means Street campus. This
the opportunity to share resources
reaching a larger, more diverse au
working on a master site plan.

purpose is to promote excellence,
orms of contemporary art. We
ort for emerging and established
nternational levels and create
ork with the public. In all aspects
is committed to gender equality
educating and cultivating
supporters, we serve as a major
utheast.

m & Video moved its offices into
boration offers both organizations
conduct joint programming
nce. The two organizations are

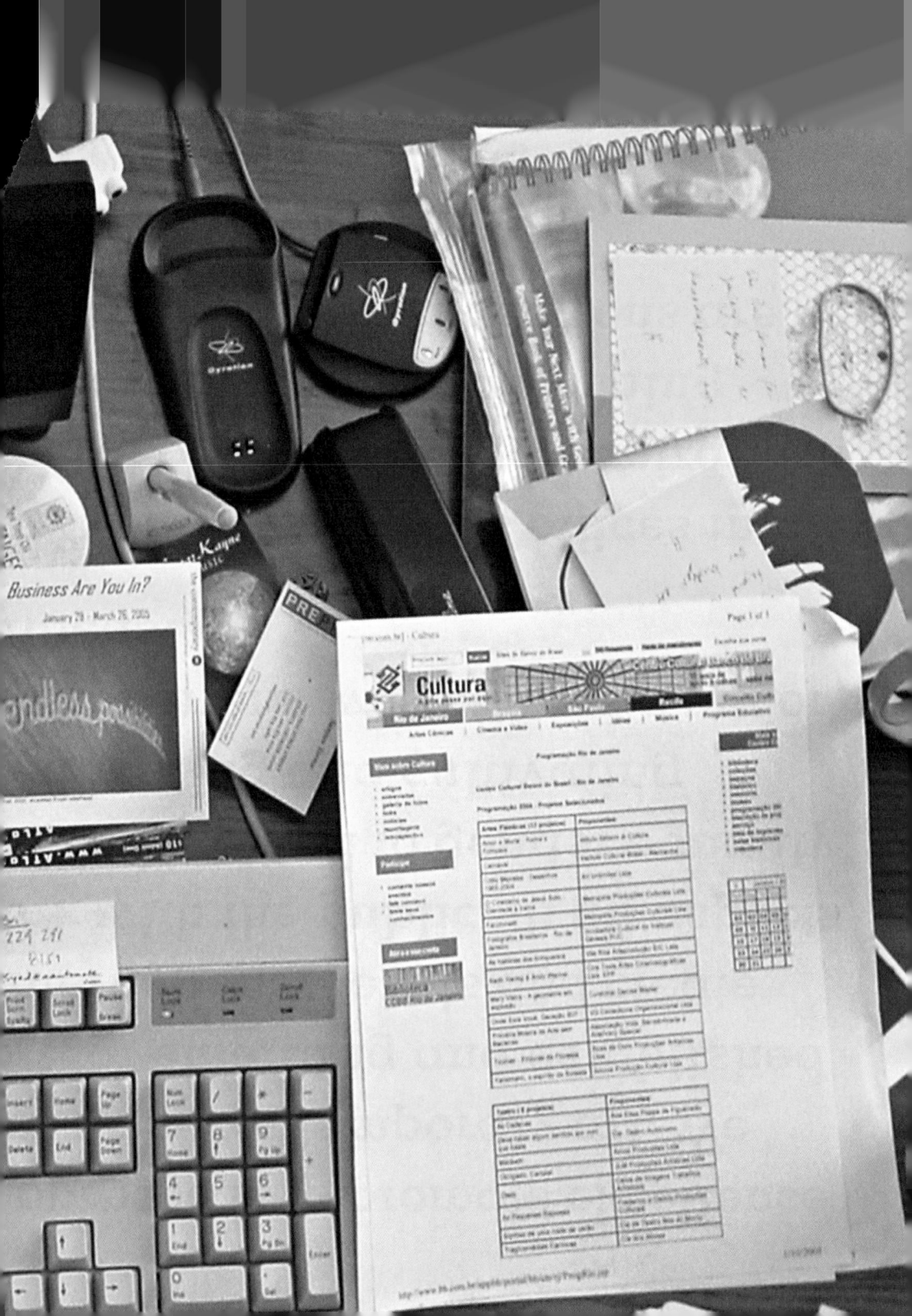

Our space. Atlanta Contemporary Arts Center.

Atlanta Contemporary Art Center
535 Means Street
Atlanta, Georgia 30318
404 688 1970
404 577 5856 fax
thecontemporary.org

Women & Their Work was founded by three women artists at the height of the artists space and women's movement. Together, they produced a city-wide, three-month long festival that featured women artists in all disciplines and was the first of its kind in Texas. Encouraged by the response to the festival, the founders decided to formalize the project by creating an art organization and Women & Their Work was born.

The changes that resulted from our participation in the Warhol Initiative have been transformative. Consultants funded by the grant allowed us to dramatically improve the efficacy of our board. The Initiative also provided us with a cash reserve. The value of a reserve is indescribable; it establishes confidence and security, and a strong base on which to build.

The mission of Women & T
develop greater recognitior
contribution to culture; pro
support for artists; present
exhibitions that reflect the
in the region; and educate
contemporary art.

: Work is to promote and

d appreciation of women's

financial and technical

ovative performances and

nic and cultural diversity

iences of all ages about

Our space. Center for Women & Their Work.

Center for Women & Their Work
1710 Lavaca Street
Austin, Texas 78701
512 477 1064
512 477 1090 fax
womenandtheirwork.org

The Center for Exploratory and Perceptual Arts (CEPA Gallery) is an artist-run art center located in the historic Market Arcade building in Buffalo, NY. It has become a national leader in supporting and showcasing photo-related art, while also serving as a research and educational center for the exploration of new technologies in the photographic arts.

The Warhol Initiative has had a tremendous impact on all of CEPA Gallery's business and managerial functions. Creation of the organization's business and marketing plan along with staff and board training proved to be invaluable in this unstable economy. CEPA Gallery has grown and stabilized over the past few years due to the peer support, access to nationally acclaimed consultants, and prestige that accompanied this high profile award. The organization is stronger, more accountable, and better prepared to face the future with confidence and optimism.

CEPA was founded in 1974 as a reso
presentation of photography and a
supports, encourages, and funds th
emerging visual artists, and is com
that have been traditionally underre
scope is international, providing a
the world. At the same time, CEPA e
New York region, which we define a
Erie, Genesee, Niagara, Orleans, an
of the Tuscarora and Seneca Nation

for the creation, education, and
d photographic arts. The gallery
bjects of both established and
d to supporting artists from groups
ented in cultural spaces. CEPA's
 for artists and curators throughout
its work by artists in the Western
egheny, Cattaraugus, Chautauqua,
oming counties and the territories

Paradise in Search of a Future Part 2. Exhibition,
Deborah Bright, 2001.

CEPA Gallery
617 Main Street #201
Buffalo, New York 14203
716 856 2717
716 270 0184 fax
cepagallery.com

Creative Time commissions, produces, and presents adventurous, temporary public artworks of all disciplines throughout New York City, offering the public rare encounters with contemporary art that enhance the everyday experience.

Where to begin? It would be an understatement to say that the Warhol Initiative stabilized our infrastructure, because it propelled forward our internal and external communications, built stronger public projects and brought our audiences closer to artists than ever. This occurred through rare support for technology upgrades, a new graphic identity, a re-designed and more dynamic website, our first ever membership program, and a new editions program helping us to strengthen our bottom line.

Creative Time bec
first presenter of te
public realm, carv
artists to engage w
multidisciplinary
musicians, architec
performance artist
well as visual artis

ne New York City's
porary art in the
g out space for
n and working with
ists including
fashion designers,
filmmakers, as

Tribute in Light. A project originally produced by John Bennett, Gustavo Bonevardi, Richard Nash Gould, Julian LaVerdiere, Paul Marantz and Paul Myoda, Creative Time and the Municipal Art Society.

Creative Time
307 Seventh Avenue
Suite 1904
New York, New York 10001
212 206 6674
212 255 8467 fax
creativetime.org

Dieu Donné Papermill is an artist workspace dedicated to the creation, promotion and preservation of contemporary art in hand-made paper.

Dieu Donné was able to use some of the Initiative funds to upgrade computers and to set up an accounting system for tracking expenses. The majority of funds is still in reserve and will be used in part to hire a consultant to run a capital campaign, raising funds to move our operation to an expanded space. The Initiative has been essential to visualize the future growth of the organization.

DIEU
DONNÉ
PAPERMILL
GALLERY
DIEU DONNE PAPERMILL & GALL
RICHARD HUNGERF

Dieu Donné was founded
paper has an untapped po
The organization began a
be recycled and explored t
art in handmade paper. T
have artists who did not t
medium work collaborativ
The energy and inventiven
the field of contemporary

he belief that handmade
tial as an art medium.
studio where ideas could
ugh the process of making
studio was equipped to
rally use paper as their
with skilled papermakers.
that resulted transformed
in paper.

Our space. Dieu Donné Papermill.

Dieu Donné Papermill
433 Broome Street
New York, New York 10013
212 226 0573
212 226 6088 fax
dieudonne.org

DiverseWorks is a non-profit art center dedicated to presenting new visual, performing, and literary arts. DiverseWorks is a place where the process of creating art is valued and where artists can test new ideas in the public arena. By encouraging the investigation of current artistic, cultural and social issues, DiverseWorks builds, educates, and sustains audiences for contemporary art.

Since DiverseWorks received the support of the Warhol Initiative, it has been an exciting time for us. The support of the foundation has allowed the board and the staff the time and resources to delve into our largest stabilization issue – our facility.

Now in its 23rd year, DiverseWorks continues to be an artist-inspired organization dedicated to presenting provocative new works in the visual, performing and literary arts. Founded by artists in 1982, DiverseWorks was originally situated downtown at 214 Travis and helped revitalize the Market Square area of downtown. In 1989, DiverseWorks moved six blocks north to a 1920's former cotton warehouse.

DiverseWorks serves as a forum for issues and work that have no other public outlet in Houston; playing a similar role nationally, DiverseWorks provides first-time commissioning opportunities for emerging artists and acts as a catalyst for young artists and arts organizations. The organization's support of challenging work by local artists, especially those considered too young or controversial to be featured in the city's galleries and museums, contributed to Houston's emergence as a leading art center.

DiverseWorks remains committed to nurturing other arts institutions in Houston and around the country in order to further broaden the reach of its programs. Some accomplishments include organizing the Houston Coalition for the Visual Arts, being the first fiscal agent for Project Row Houses and making a three-year commitment to commission new works by the then-fledgling theater company Infernal Bridegroom Productions. DiverseWorks recently completed a successful two year incubation with activist literary organization Voices Breaking Boundaries.

Tetelestai: Notebooks of the Black Sea. David McGee, 2003–2004

DiverseWorks
1117 East Freeway
Houston, Texas 77002
713 223 8346
713 223 4608 fax
diverseworks.org

Exit Art's mission is to create and present exhibitions and programs that explore the diversity of cultures and voices that continually shape contemporary art and ideas in America. Exit Art is also committed to bringing to public attention the work of underrecognized and emerging artists and experimenting with the convergence of film, video, performance art, music, design and visual art in its programming.

With the support of the Warhol Foundation, Exit Art was able to launch its first capital campaign, leverage other institutional funding, strengthen our overall organizational fundraising capacity, and receive strategic financial support when the organization needed it most.

Exit Art's exhibitions, pe
have frequently challeng
what art is and created
the public and the artist t
a place where artists cou
art world and enter a la
edgy art work.

mances, and programs
traditional notions of
opportunities to bring
ether. Exit Art represents
exit the mainstream
atory of experimental,

Our space. Exit Art has nearly completed renovations on its two-floor facility, a stunning facelift to Hell's Kitchen's first cultural outpost.

Exit Art
475 10th Avenue
1st Floor
New York, New York 10018
212 966 7745
212 925 2928 fax
exitart.org

The 509 Cultural Center was founded in 1987 by a multicultural, all volunteer group of Tenderloin residents (and a couple others) who lived in the Aarti Cooperative Hotel; their purpose was to establish an arts presence which supported the work of new and emerging artists from the Tenderloin and other areas.

Through the Warhol Initiative, we have been able to leverage matching funds for capitol improvement projects including the renovation of the back office where we can now store art work. Coupled with a new strategic and marketing plan, we have generated greater public awareness for the exhibition, performing and public art programs which has resulted in larger audiences, and an increase in art sales by three- to four-fold.

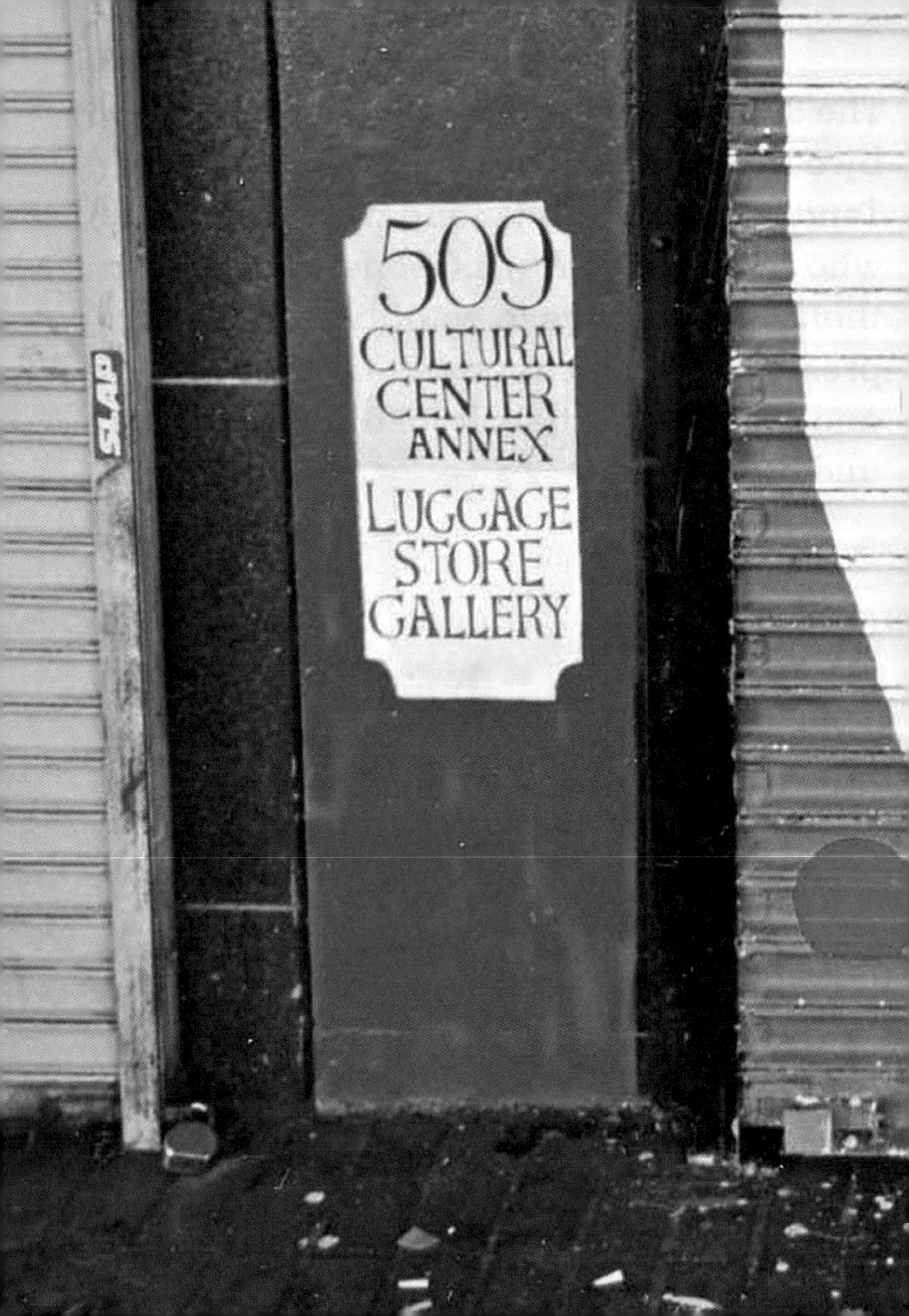
509
CULTURAL
CENTER
ANNEX
LUGGAGE
STORE
GALLERY
SLAP

In October 1989, when the ear
building housing 509 was dan
1990 and we began looking fo

We located space at 1007 Mark
Complete Luggage Store. We
Store as an interim project of
an annex. The Luggage Store
business in this location. Met
historic building says *The Co*
about The Knitting Factory an

Little did we know we would
would become home.

ake hit San Francisco, the
ed. A retrofit was planned for
interim space.

treet on the third floor of The
ned the venue, The Luggage
509 Cultural Center or
rived its name from a prior
ettering at the top of this
ete *Luggage Store*. We knew
he Kitchen in NYC, and well...

hase the building and this

Our front door. Painted by Margaret Kilgallen in 1996 as part of the *Roll Down Door Project*.

509 Cultural Center
aka The Luggage Store
1007 Market Street
San Francisco, California 94103
415 255 5971
415 863 5509 fax
luggagestoregallery.org

Galería was founded in 1970 by a group of artists active in the Chicano civil rights movement. Galería's name reflects its role as a community arts organization serving the Latino community based in San Francisco's Mission District, the neighborhood with the largest Latino population in the city. "Raza," a term of self-identification used since the Chicano civil rights movement, literally means: "our people."

Warhol support was crucial in helping Galería become a much more stable organization. Although fundraising will always be a challenge, thanks to the Initiative, we have increased earned income and developed a good foundation from which to grow.

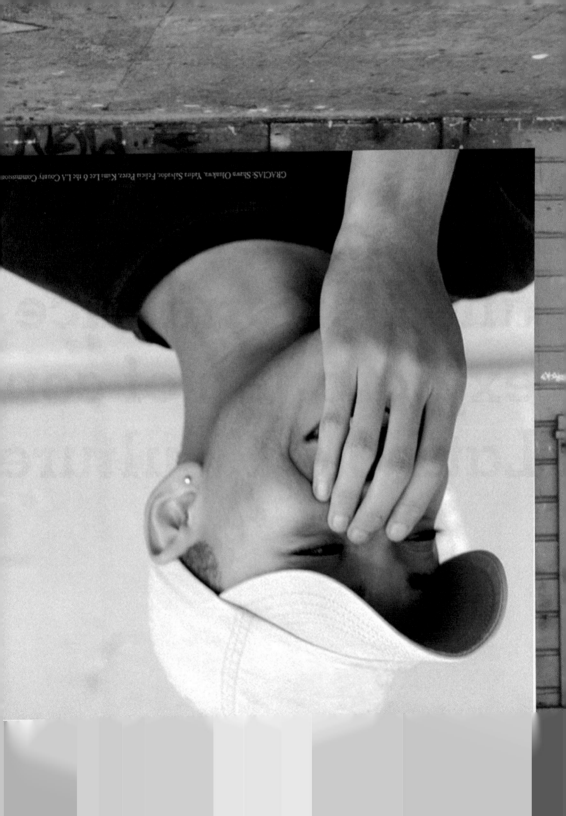

Galería's main ob
serve as a labora
of new work in th
and performance
exploration of con
Latino art, culture

ctives are to
y for the creation
isual, literary,
ts and for the
mporary issues in
nd civic society.

HOUSE OF COLOR

BARBER SHOP and BEAUTY SALON

Our space. Galería de la Raza.

Galería de la Raza
2857 24th Street
San Francisco, California 94110
415 826 8009
415 826 6235 fax
galeriadelaraza.org

Hallwalls was founded in 1974 by a group of young visual artists including Charles Clough, Nancy Dwyer, Robert Longo, and Cindy Sherman who carved an exhibition space out of the walls of the hall outside their studios in a former ice house in Buffalo. They supported and exhibited new work by local artists and created opportunities for exchange between them and artists in other cities. From the beginning, their focus was interdisciplinary. The earliest programs featured not only visual artists, but musicians, writers, filmmakers, video artists and performance artists.

The Warhol Initiative enabled us to increase an endowment fund to help stabilize Hallwalls' financial future. We were also able to address technology needs, allowing us to upgrade our systems.

The founding principles and artistic
As the various programs expanded a
they were always unified by the orga
most challenging contemporary worl

People are constantly astonished at tl
in so many different disciplines, and
achieve that with such a small core st

Today, Hallwalls is entering an exci
relocated to a refurbished church in
Righteous Babe Records (RBR). The n
foot gallery and a dual-purpose scree
has access to RBR's 1,200 capacity pe
the nave in the former church.

egies continue to guide Hallwalls.
ew in distinctly different directions,
on's mission to bring the newest and
ie public.

lume and range of our programming
ially by the fact that we are able to
nd on such a relatively small budget.

new stage of development. We have
town Buffalo, sharing space with
renovated facility has a 2,500-square-
/performance space. Hallwalls
nance space occupying what was

Hallwalls staff. On the roof of their temporary quarters on Delaware Avenue with their future home across the street in the background. Carl Lee, Joanna Raczynska, Polly Little, John Massier, Edmund Cardoni.

Hallwalls Contemporary Arts Center
341 Delaware Avenue
Buffalo, New York 14202
716 854 1694
hallwalls.org

Headlands Center for the Arts was conceived during a planning process for transfer of abandoned former military property to the National Park Service. A group composed primarily of local artists successfully advocated for the inclusion of an art center on the site. They addressed the historic rehabilitation of our buildings in Fort Barry as a site-specific creative project, inspiring the development of the community and activities that make up the Headlands today.

The recognition that came with the Initiative meant a lot to internal morale and externally helped us promote ourselves. Initiative funding gave us the ability to advance technologically by purchasing new equipment for the artists and staff, upgrading Internet, email and digital capabilities and developing our first professional website. The Initiative also enabled us to set up our first Working Capital Reserve, which has proven invaluable and led to firmer financial footing for the organization.

For Headlands Center for the Arts, the first years were devoted to renovating the long-abandoned buildings and raising funds. In 1986, the Center hired its first Director with seed funding from the San Francisco Foundation. HCA successfully expanded its programs by leveraging other support from government, corporations, foundations and individuals.

In 1994, the Center reached another milestone when it signed a 20-year Cooperative Agreement with the National Park Service. HCA exists today as part of a family of non-profit cultural and environmental organizations in the Golden Gate National Recreation Area. The Center's unique approach to its site, which involved artists and volunteers in transforming the dilapidated historic structures, gave birth to an experiment in community and collaboration which influences its work today. Not only have the buildings themselves become works of art, but in the past 18 years, HCA has built a wide variety of dynamic programs, including artists' residencies, lectures, performances, publications, community-based projects and commissions.

Headlands Center for the Arts now manages ten buildings, offers a mix of residencies and studio use to artists from dozens of countries, and provides the public with a wide variety of dynamic programs, including artists' residencies, lectures, performances, publications, community-based projects and commissions. More than 1,000 artists from such diverse places as Croatia, Israel, Sweden, Taiwan, and our own Bay Area have come to HCA to live and work together. Public programs involve hundreds each year in dialogue with artists and creative thinkers from many other disciplines, and HCA enjoys the support of more than 500 members and donors.

Yu Wen-Fu. Artist in Residence, 2002.

Headlands Center for the Arts
944 Fort Barry
Sausalito, California 94965
415 331 2787
415 331 3857 fax
headlands.org

Since 1973, Intermedia Arts has been a place where our innovative approach to the arts has inspired communities toward social change. We are nationally recognized for our position in the community, successful education and leadership programs, unique services to artists, and multidisciplinary public exhibitions.

Intermedia Arts experienced radical development over the period of the Warhol Initiative. We hired a new executive director and restructured the organization's management to a cross-functional team approach, which encouraged new leadership throughout the organization. Intermedia Arts' programming has become dramatically more focused. The Warhol funds created important financial management opportunities as well as desperately needed technological infrastructure improvements.

The mission of Intermedia A
understanding among peopl
to foster excellence in the cre
presenting diverse cultural p
in which those multiple persp
can ultimately bring people t
that lead to new relationship
strengthen the quality of life

s to be a catalyst that builds
rough art. It is our intention
ve process and product by
pectives. We create a context
ives can be understood and
ther. We stimulate dialogues
d connections that, in turn,
all communities.

The view from our window. Intermedia Arts.

Intermedia Arts
2822 Lyndale Avenue South
Minneapolis, Minnesota 55408
612 871 4444
612 871 6927 fax
intermediaarts.org

On March 5, 1975 a large group of artists gathered in the studio of local artists Philomene Bennett and Lou Marak to address *How the Artist Can Benefit From Centralization.* Overwhelmingly the group felt a self-initiated organization was the only alternative to isolation, elitism, apathy, and ignorance. The ultimate result of that meeting was the formation of the Kansas City Artist Coalition.

In 2002 KCAC was honored to accept the Warhol Initiative Award from the Andy Warhol Foundation for the Visual Arts. The grant has been used to upgrade technology and create a working capital cash reserve to ensure the stability of KCAC in future years.

ARKA
KARA

KARA

The exhibitions and programs o
reflect the rich artistic, cultural
in our city, state, and nation. KC
in their quest to realize their vi
innovative and experimental art
to commercial venues. KCAC is
community and continues to be

Focusing on emerging and mid-
often provides these artists with
opportunity. The exhibitions hel
and make it possible for the ge
learn about contemporary art.

Kansas City Artists Coalition
ethnic diversity that exists
s desire is to support all artists
. KCAC is also a space for
ich does not readily lend itself
voice of inclusion in our
rimary support for local artists.

er artists from the region, KCAC
ir first important exhibition
vance their professional careers
l public to experience and

Bumper Sticker. Kansas City Artists Coalition, circa 1985.

Kansas City Artists Coalition
201 Wyandotte
Kansas City, Missouri 64105
816 421 5222
816 421 0656 fax
kansascityartistscoalition.org

Legion Arts is an artist-run organization that promotes new and innovative expression in the visual, performing, literary, and electronic arts; fosters creative interaction between artists, their communities and society; and encourages the imaginative exploration of contemporary ideas and experience.

Our involvement in the Warhol Initiative came at a truly critical time for the organization. Infrastructure and systems desperately needed shoring up. Programs needed examination and clarification. Most importantly, the structure, priorities and future direction of the founder-run company needed to be addressed in a broad, systematic and clear-headed manner. While challenges remain in each of these areas, great progress has been made. It's no exaggeration at all to say that this progress would not have been possible without the Warhol Initiative.

For Legion Arts, the
is making connecti
and often unpredict
artist to audience,
one another, the ind
ideas and experien
to new ways of exp
and their concerns.

ost important work

s that are positive

le: artist to artist,

trary audiences to

dual to divergent

, and communities

sing themselves

Bosnian artist Paco Rosic. At work on a spray paint mural for

Opening reception. At CSPS, tents and paintings by artist Dan Attoe.

Legion Arts
1103 Third Street SE
Cedar Rapids, Iowa 52401
319 364 1580
319 362 9156 fax
legionarts.org

LACE works collaboratively with artists and serves as a laboratory for creative expression. The result is work that challenges traditional assumptions about art and the exhibition-making process, pushes the envelope in terms of engaging with its audience, and in some ways, "de-mystifies" the creative process itself.

The Warhol Initiative has made every difference as LACE has moved from a crisis-management mode into one of forward-thinking planning and strategic growth. The Warhol Initiative has had a profound impact on LACE and its future.

Uniquely positioned amo
and major art institutions
Exhibitions (LACE) has a
the field of contemporary
itself by serving as a lab
and creative expression
collaborations among ar
audiences that are centr
projects we produce.

commercial galleries
s Angeles Contemporary
gnificant role to play in
t. LACE distinguishes
tory for artistic research
artists, facilitating
s, the organization, and
o the exhibitions and

Los Angeles Contemporary Exhibitions
6522 Hollywood Boulevard
Los Angeles, California 90028
323 957 1777
323 957 9025 fax
artleak.org

MACLA is a contemporary arts space where Latino artists create and showcase new work in the visual, literary and performance arts to help define, interpret and transform society.

Since receiving the grant from the Warhol Initiative, MACLA has changed tremendously. What it means to have a working capital cash reserve cannot be measured. For an organization in its 15th year, the reserve and the training on how best to use it was invaluable for us. In addition, the chance to interact and learn from similar organizations has greatly improved our ability to transform and meet the changes in the communities we serve and represent.

Free Admission

Gallery Hours: Wednesday & Thursday, 12noon – 7pm
Friday & Saturday, 12noon – 5pm

Exhibition: March 18 – April 20, 2005

the CHICANA/O Bie...

Movimiento de Arte y Cultura Latino A...

MACLA is often described

A three-tiered approach

programming philosophy

artists throughout all leve

an expansive cross-ethni

a hybrid aesthetic vision

elements of popular cultu

with established and trad

s a "workshop of culture."
nes the organization's
st, support for emerging
of programming; second,
ensibility; and third,
mfortable with mixing
nd sociological interests
onal art forms.

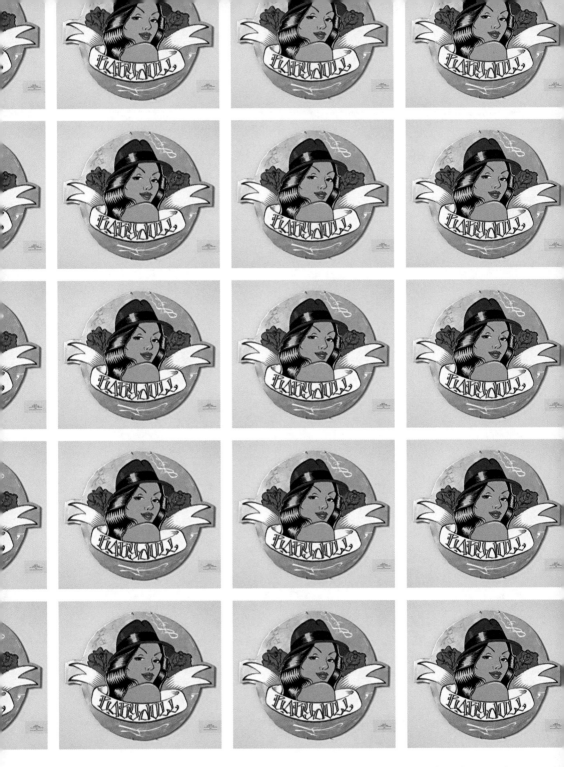

Babydoll. Abraham Ortega, one shot enamel on aluminum from the collection of Imelda Gonzalez.

MACLA/Movimiento de Arte y
Cultura Latino Americana
510 First Street
San Jose, California 95113
408 287 7174
408 998 2814 fax
maclaarte.org

New Langton Arts was founded in 1975 in San Francisco's South of Market district by a group of artists and arts professionals in response to the lack of opportunities to present their ideas and artwork. Their goal was to create an artist-run space, a place for the production and presentation of experimental artwork where community members, artists, and audiences could participate.

Since receiving a grant from the Warhol Initiative, New Langton Arts has made significant progress in its efforts to relocate to a new facility. The board of directors formed the Building and Planning Committee to oversee all aspects of the relocation process. In 2002, Langton completed its first strategic plan with the assistance of a consulting team. A year later, Langton and another organization, SF Camerawork, completed a facilities business plan exploring co-location options. In 2004, both organizations began working with a real estate firm, and continue to work with them in search of appropriate properties.

The mission of New Langton A

and innovative contemporary

music, performance, literature

while encouraging public app

of our times. The organization

contemporary artists from dive

backgrounds through exhibitio

works commissions, awards, an

to further experience Langton'

outreach, and audience develo

s to cultivate experimental
 in the visual and media arts,
 interdisciplinary media,
ation of and access to the art
ides professional support to
economic, social, and cultural
performances, readings, new
ablications. Audiences are able
 ist projects with education,
ent programs.

The Problem with Poodles. Tamara Fites, mixed media installation, 2003.

New Langton Arts
1246 Folsom Street
San Francisco, California 94103
415 626 5416
415 225 1453 fax
newlangtonarts.org

911 Media Arts Center supports the creative use of media in communication and artistic expression. Our mission is to promote the diversity of voices in our community by providing the resources necessary for artists to create, exhibit, and distribute independent media to local audiences and beyond. We believe that everyone can and should have access to the tools of communication.

For the first time in our 21 year history, we have a member-elected Board of Trustees that collectively provides leadership and fundraising skills for the organization. Through the Initiative's strategic planning assistance, board development process, and 911's decision to use substantial funds for a cash reserve, we have created a strong foundation from which we continue to build a truly sustainable organization.

As a direct result of the strategic planning process, and with funding support from Warhol, we renovated and moved to a new facility in 2004. The new space offers significantly reduced overhead, and it gave us the chance to design the facility in a way that better serves our artists, audiences, and local community.

The objectives of 911 Media Arts
access to state-of-the-art digital
sional training in media product
video, animation, and web-base
venues for exhibition and discus
dent media-makers; support arti
art, technology, and mass media
contemporary culture; and foster
ment in youth, by promoting self
through critical creative analysi

r are to: give artists affordable
a equipment; provide profes-
including all aspects of digital
horing; offer superior public
of work by artists and indepen-
nquiry, exploring the fusion of
l its impact on our society and
c dialogue and artistic develop-
rmination and empowerment
l hands-on production.

View from our window. Seattle's Space Needle framed in 911's front window.

911 Media Arts
402 9th Avenue North
Seattle, Washington 98109
206 682 6552
206 682 7422 fax
911media.org

Out North was established in 1985 to create opportunities for Alaskans to gather and share new and more innovative artwork than was typically found in the state. The aim was to provide a forum for artists who were not supported by other organizations in the region.

Through the Initiative program, our staff and board learned that we're not alone in supporting essential, non-commercial art and artists in a market-valued economy. More concretely, Out North set up a server network and purchased critical equipment for our media program that has led to a growing audience for independent media. We have also completed a strategic plan and created operating reserves. Finally, we began preparations to build affordable artist housing/studios and finalized negotiations to purchase the 10,000-square foot facility we have leased from the local government for 13 years.

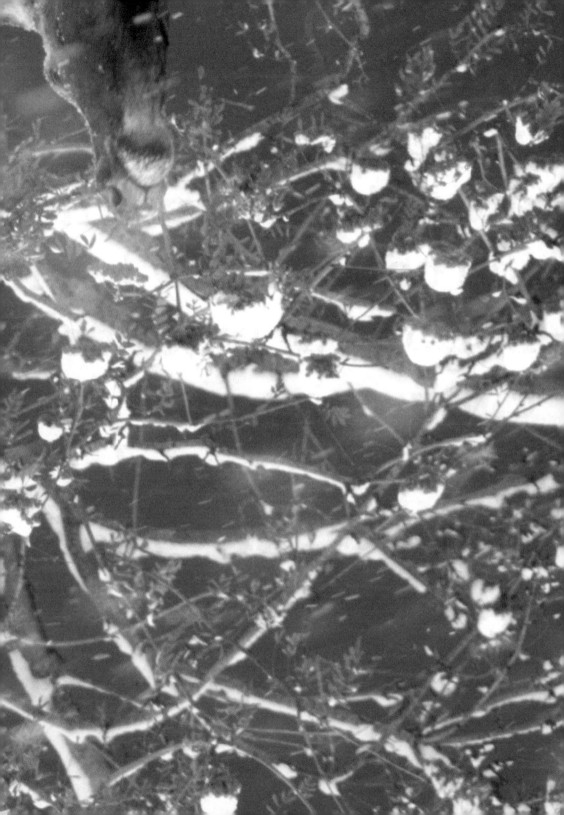

Out North exhibits th
visual, performing ar
organization creates
the community to cho
notions of what cons
culture, and presents
platform for underse
and audiences.

vork of contemporary
media artists. The
nd connects art with
enge conventional
utes contemporary
n artist-focused
ed artists, art forms,

The view from our window. Out North.

Photo by: Bob Hallinen / Anchorage Daily News

Out North
3800 DeBarr Road
Anchorage, Alaska 99508
907 279 8099
907 279 8100 fax
outnorth.org

Project Row Houses was founded in 1993 as a result of discussions among African-American artists who wanted to establish a positive, creative presence in their own community. Artist and community activist Rick Lowe pursued this vision when he discovered the abandoned 1½ block site of 22 shotgun-style houses in Houston's Third Ward and was inspired by their historical and cultural ties to Freedman's Town communities found throughout the South.

The Warhol Initiative grant allowed us to pay off our mortgage so we own our property free and clear, allowing us the opportunity to pay off other debts and start a cash reserve.

The mission of Project R
community through the
African-American histor
is founded in public art
encompass neighborhoo
preservation, and comm
of a community of shotg
unique environment for
engage our visitors in th
celebrate African-Amer
and address educationa

Houses is to create
ebration of the arts and
nd culture. Our work
ucation programs that
evitalization, historic
ty service. The setting
houses provides a
creation of works that
reative process,
n history and culture,
nd community needs.

After school program. Supported by Project Row Houses.

Project Row Houses
2500 Holman Street
P.O. Box 1001
Houston, Texas 77251
713 526 7662
713 526 1623 fax
projectrowhouses.org

Real Art Ways is an alternative, multi-disciplinary arts organization that presents and supports contemporary artists and their work, facilitates the creation of new work, and creatively engages and informs audiences and communities.

With assistance from the Warhol Initiative program, we have increased support from individuals, corporations and foundations. We were also able to set up a cash reserve and an endowment, and increase earned income from ticket sales dramatically.

Real Art Ways p[r]
support alternati[ve]
artistic points of [view]
audiences as an [...]
the work. The org[...]
contemporary art[...]
established artis[ts...]
culturally and ec[...]
community.

ides space to
and challenging
w and to engage
tegral part of
nization presents
y emerging and
and serves a
omically diverse

Creative Cocktail Hour. Pontani Sisters, 2002.

Real Art Ways
56 Arbor Street
Hartford, Connecticut 06106
860 232 1006
860 233 6691 fax
realartways.org

The Salina Art Center was founded by artists, educators, and community members who envisioned a gallery and education center in North-Central Kansas. The Art Center was housed originally in the Kansas Wesleyan University campus.

The Warhol Initiative provided the catalyst for the Salina Art Center to stabilize our organization while stimulating our work with artists. The Art Center embarked on a campaign to establish an artist initiative fund, renovate a warehouse in downtown Salina for artist residences and studios, and to build our endowment. The grant from the Warhol Foundation allowed us to launch a campaign in our community that has furthered our mission of creating exchanges among art, artists, and audiences, all the while undergirding our operations and facilities with more predictable annual endowment income.

The mission of the Sali
exchanges among art,
The founders wanted t
educational facility tho
the whole community
art, in Salina and beyo

Art Center is to create
ists, and audiences.
stablish a gallery and
neant something to
l created a center for

Salina Art Center staff. Minus a few key players.

Salina Art Center
242 South Santa Fe
P.O. Box 743
Salina, Kansas 67402
785 827 1431
785 827 0686 fax
salinaartcenter.org

SF Camerawork is an arts organization that encourages emerging and mid-career artists to explore new directions in photography and related media. The organization fosters creative forms of expressions that push existing boundaries.

Since receiving a grant from the Warhol Initiative, SF Camerawork's cash reserve has expanded to provide a strong foundation financially. The Initiative also enabled us to complete a significant strategic planning and facility planning process, which helped prepare us for the next major step in our organizational development – acquiring a permanent facility.

SF Camerawork was
promote photography
expression. Through e
and educational prog
stimulates public dia
contemporary image-
of current social and

ablished in 1976 to
a medium of artistic
ibitions, publications
ms, SF Camerawork
ue and inquiry about
king in the context
thetic issues.

Agitate: Negotiating the Photographic Process.
Installation view, 2003.

SF Camerawork
1246 Folsom Street
San Francisco, California 94103
415 863 1001
415 863 1015 fax
sfcamerawork.org

Located in East Los Angeles, Self-Help Graphics & Art was originally formed as an artist collective in 1972. The purpose of the organization is to build community through art and culture.

Self-Help Graphics & Art has changed since receiving the Warhol grant. Positive changes have resulted from the support; negative changes were due to the funding climate and damage to our building. It is so critically important to note that we would not have been in a position to manage these changes if we had not had the support from the Initiative. Even in the clouds, you can see blue skies if you have the vision.

The mission of Self-
to serve local artists
and a range of audi
Chicano and Latino
of the American lan
and a printshop, its
exhibitions, worksh
with other communi
archive program.

p Graphics & Art is
ne local community
es by presenting
and culture as part
ape. With a gallery
ograms include
, artist exchanges
s, and now, an

Self-Help Graphics building. Created by Roberto Gutierrez.

Self-Help Graphics & Art
3802 Cesar E. Chavez Avenue
Los Angeles, California 90063
323 264 1259
323 881 6447 fax
selfhelpgraphics.com

Located in San Francisco's Mission District, Southern Exposure is dedicated to supporting emerging artists and arts educators. The organization presents experimental, cutting-edge contemporary art exhibitions and innovative arts education programs, and provides a space where the two intersect.

With support from the Warhol Initiative, Southern Exposure has fundamentally become a stronger organization. Southern Exposure's financial base has been solidified through the establishment of a working capital cash reserve followed by the reorganization and upgrade of our financial infrastructure. We are also planning, preparing, and fundraising for a major long-term capital improvement project. Through the completion of a three-year strategic plan that reflects the organization's priorities as well as those of the communities we serve, we have been able to make significant progress on these and other goals.

Southern Exposure has b
innovative art and comm
As an artist-run organiza
reaches out to diverse au
forum and resource cente
arts and education comm
Programs include visual
ing artists, as well as ev
Education Program (AIE)
high school students to p
programs.

presenting dynamic,
ity programs since 1974.
n, Southern Exposure
ences, and serves as a
roviding support to the
ities in the Bay Area.
s exhibitions by emerg-
s, and the Artists in
nich allows hundreds of
icipate in art-related

Our space. Southern Exposure.

Southern Exposure
401 Alabama Street
San Francisco, California 94110
415 863 2141
415 863 1841 fax
soex.org

Space One Eleven was founded in 1986 in Birmingham, Alabama to address the isolation experienced by artists in the region who had little access to art resources and opportunities. The organization takes its name from its original street address. Space One Eleven is now located in the midst of urban Birmingham's historic core—a neighborhood cited in the 1990 census as the poorest zip code in the United States, an area now home to a racially diverse, mixed income federal housing project.

The working capital cash reserve from the Warhol Initiative has contributed towards Space One Eleven's sustainability. The grant encouraged board members to play an increasingly active role in the organization.

Space One Eleven enc
of Birmingham's comp
the exploration of new
for the future. Deeply
organization's mission
opportunities for visua
for public understandi
and offer arts educatic

ages the investigation
ated past as well as
odels of social justice
ounded in place, the
o provide professional
rtists, create a forum
 of contemporary art,
o area youth.

BAMA. 2004 Exhibition, contained new installations by Jane Timberlake, Annie Kammerer Butrus, and Amy Pleasant. Timberlake and Pleasant were then picked by Helena Reckitt to be included in the Atlanta Biennale.

Space One Eleven
2409 Second Avenue North
Birmingham, Alabama 35203
205 328 0553
205 254 6176 fax
spaceoneeleven.org

SPACES is an artist-run organization founded in 1978 as an alternative to commercial galleries and museums. It seeks to advance the artist's vision by providing artists with resources, space, an audience and the freedom to engage the public in a dialogue about contemporary art.

With the Warhol Initiative grant, SPACES has gained financial stability, and has received recognition and validation on a local, national and international level. By paying off our remaining mortgage debt, the grant freed up funds to create a new program, the SPACES World Artists Program, that enabled us to significantly expand our work with artists and the community. We are part of a network of peer Warhol Initiative groups that communicate regularly.

SPACES champions
boundaries with ch
The organization er
experiment with ne
and innovative use
newly created SPAC
Program, it now has
program that bring
national artist to Cl

rtists who push
enging new ideas.
ourages them to
forms of expression
f media. With the
S World Artists
n artist residency
ational and inter-
eland.

Our space. Rooftop sign sculpture by Xan Palay.

SPACES
2220 Superior Viaduct
Cleveland, Ohio 44113
216 621 2314
216 621 2314 fax
spacesgallery.org

Through exhibitions, a curated slide and video file, and public programs, White Columns creates a forum for presenting new work by emerging and underrepresented artists.

The Warhol Initiative grant increased our cash reserve fund and significantly bolstered both our long-term security and growth, while relieving an enormous amount of pressure that results from our seasonal cash flow. As a result, we have been able to program with the confidence that we will meet basic expenses, avoiding having to solicit emergency contributions from board members. Additionally, the technology grant greatly expanded the support we can offer to emerging and underrepresented artists in our Curated Artists Registry.

Founded in 1969, White Colum
collaboration of artists who we
and displaying art. As an alter
exhibits and supports provoca
It develops programs that enc
between generations of artists
general public.

tarted as a loosely organized
xploring new ways of making
ve venue, White Columns
 and new contemporary art.
ge dialogue between artists,
d between the artist and the

Back office. Amie Scally and Rebecca Gee.

White Columns
320 West 13th Street
New York, New York 10014
212 924 4212
212 645 4764 fax
whitecolumns.org

Artspace was originally founded by a group of New Haven-based visual and performing artists in response to the elimination of a promised gallery space dedicated to local artists in a prominent local theater. Convinced that local visual art and performance needed an alternative showcase, they created Artspace. Artspace's mission is to connect artists, audiences, and resources; to catalyze artistic activity; and to redefine art spaces.

With the benefit of the Warhol grant, we hope to update and streamline our financial operations, record keeping and data management, and create a platform for the eventual expansion of our space to a site that we own. In sum, we hope the Warhol Initiative will help us through our growing pains!

The name Artspace originally d
black box reserved for local arti
never delivered by the Shubert
became an umbrella for a varie
having a permanent home. We
Artspace while operating witho
found spaces as art spaces. So
factory buildings (including for
corsets, cash registers, and Erec
schools, public greenways, city
Today, we actually have a semi-
a lease and rent payments and o
have come full circle. We mount
and also continue to seek out o
alternative venues.

ibed the permanent space and
nd performers, promised but
ts next incarnation, the name
projects built around NOT
d the irony of using the name
space, and instead claiming
our "artspaces" have included
manufacturers of tires, rifles,
Sets), public libraries, public
s, and old malls and storefronts.
nanent space, complete with
essions, so in a certain way, we
cycles of exhibitions annually
tunities for artists to exhibit in

Our space. Though Artspace only leases the first floor of this building, the former Chamberlain Furniture factory, we got permission to paint our name on the upper façade.

Artspace
50 Orange Street
New Haven, Connecticut 06510
203 772 2709
203 772 0850 fax
artspacenh.org

Aurora Picture Show was established in 1998 by two Houston-based media artists. Through volunteer labor and equipment donations, the two converted a 1924 wooden church building into a 100-seat capacity cinema. Aurora's mandate from the start was to champion artist-made films and videos, to host visiting film/videomakers and curators, and to encourage active audiences.

At present, our staff wears many hats and performs courageous acts of load balancing. We hope that the Warhol Initiative will assist in finding resourceful ways to alleviate some of the heavy workload on our staff and volunteers. We sense that the Initiative self-assessment process will help us define the strengths of each staff, board member, and volunteer, and use those more effectively. Most importantly, Aurora is in a tremendous growth period and seeks to fiercely hold on to our original vision while expanding our programs, artists services and mission.

Aurora Picture S
independent fil
media artists, th
exhibition oppo
artist fees. A hy
art space, reside
Aurora is the on
kind in the Sout

ow supports
video and new
ough promotion,
unities, and
id microcinema,
ce, and church,
venue of its
vest.

Sparkle Box. Video sculpture by Andy Mann. This runs 24 hours per day outside of Aurora Picture Show.

Aurora Picture Show
800 Aurora Street
Houston, Texas 77009
713 868 2101
aurorapictureshow.org

Franklin Art Works is a multidisciplinary alternative space devoted to presenting new work by leading local, national and international artists. Over the past five years we have grown to present 15 one-person exhibitions annually in three galleries accompanied by collaborative events in performance, music, film and readings.

We have been greatly energized by the opportunities presented by the Warhol Initiative, including the means to complete a comprehensive strategic plan, increase staff, upgrade equipment and further develop our board of directors. With a more developed infrastructure we look forward to enhancing our national stature and increasing our overall service to artists and our community.

Franklin Art Works is loca
Minneapolis in the city's
neighborhood. With the o
10,000-square-foot facility
theater, Franklin Art Worl
for artistic innovation and

l adjacent to downtown
t culturally diverse
ing development of our
ormer silent-era movie
s creating a dynamic site
cial interaction.

Our space. Franklin Art Works.

Franklin Art Works
1021 East Franklin Avenue
Minneapolis, Minnesota 55404
612 872 7494
612 872 7403 fax
franklinartworks.org

Locust Projects was founded in 1998 by three artists living in Miami who recognized the need for an alternative art venue. They created an exhibition space that presents visual art to the public.

Locust Projects expects to continue to do great things with the support of the Warhol Initiative. Locust Projects is ready to bring the organization to the next level of growth to enhance all aspects of its administrative and programmatic development, e.g., staffing, facilities improvement and technology expansion. The Initiative Funding will enhance the opportunities we provide for our artists and help to strengthen the organization's foundation.

Locust Projects is a p
encouraged to exper
or methods without
sales or the limitati
exhibition spaces. P
given a significant t
out their projects in
are realized on site,
of the creative proce
an extension of the

ce where artists are
ent with new ideas
nking about gallery
s of conventional
icipating artists are
e period to work
e space. The shows
d due to the nature
, the projects are
ist's typical work.

Locust Projects staff. Westen Charles, Gean Moreno & Cooper.

Locust Projects
105 NW 23rd Street
Miami, Florida 33127
305 576 8570
locustprojects.org

Midway Contemporary Art is committed to encouraging innovation and diversity in the visual arts. A public platform, Midway supports emerging and underrepresented artists, contributes toward significant new developments in the field, and stimulates the ongoing public discourse of art and culture.

The Warhol Initiative will enable Midway to develop into a more sustainable organization that is better able to serve our artists. We hope to utilize the program to increase our staffing and implement formal structures and processes for our board of directors and staff. We believe that this will enable us to not only strengthen our current programming, but also allow us to move forward with new forms of programming.

Each year Midway works w
facilitating the production
in the Twin Cities. In four y
26 exhibitions that have fea
artists. Our one- and two-p
new projects from emergin
had this type of substantial
of their work. For our larger
the selection has been more
exhibited established and

a new selection of artists,
 premiere of new artwork
s, we have developed
ed, in total, more than 120
on exhibitions facilitate
rtists who often have not
sentation and consideration
ematic group exhibitions,
ergenerational as we have
erging artists together.

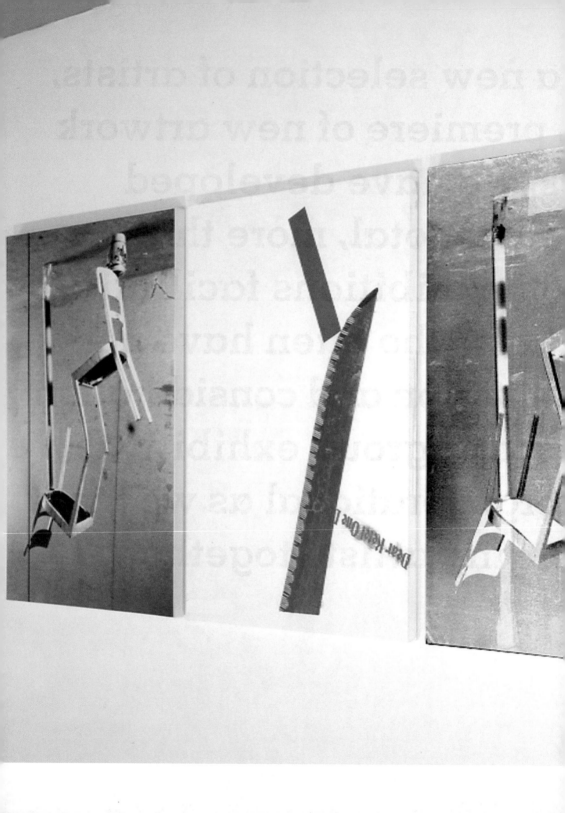

View from our windows. Midway Contemporary Art.

Midway Contemporary Art
3338 University Avenue SE, #400
Minneapolis, Minnesota 55414
612 605 4504
612 605 4538 fax
midwayart.org

Momenta Art is an exhibition space located in Williamsburg, Brooklyn. Its mission is to promote the work of emerging artists, primarily through two-person shows, providing an opportunity for the artists to present a substantial body of work.

Momenta Art and its neighborhood of Williamsburg, Brooklyn have developed strong cultural reputations over the past ten years. By working with the Warhol Initiative, Momenta will work to ensure its cultural capital by stabilizing its facilities within a rapidly developing community. The gallery will also work with the Initiative to develop our board and expand our staff, ensuring that the gallery can take full advantage of all opportunities for growth.

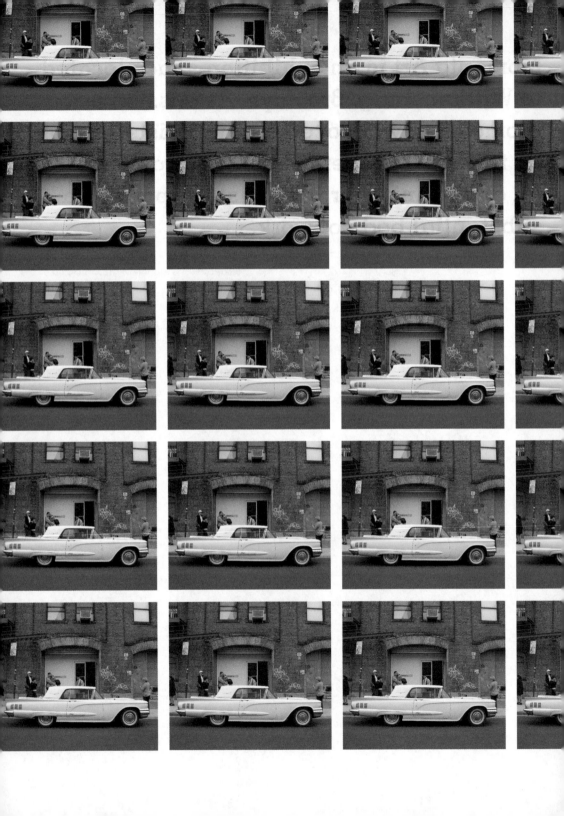

Momenta Art was originally
in 1986. Six years later, the
New York City, functioning
as a migratory gallery whil
a variety of temporary venu
of 1995, Momenta Art reoper
space in Brooklyn. Its progr
publications such as newsle
multiples, and an annual fu

ablished in Philadelphia
nization relocated to
ng the transitional phase
esenting exhibitions in
n Manhattan. In the spring
in a permanent exhibition
include exhibitions,
s and limited edition artist
aiser.

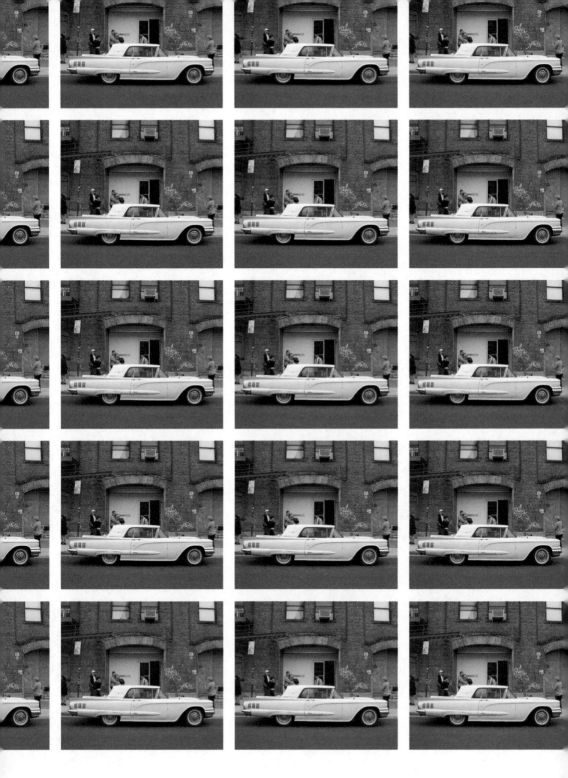

Momenta Art
72 Berry Street
Brooklyn, New York 11211
718 218 8058
momentaart.org

PARTICIPANT INC seeks to provide a venue in which artists, curators, writers, and educators can develop, realize, and present ambitious projects within a context that recognizes the social and cultural value of artistic experimentation.

The Warhol Initiative poses an invaluable challenge to our organization to think beyond our day-to-day survival and to consider, instead, the long-term sustainability of PARTICIPANT INC. Stability for our staff increases our ability to think about the future and the ways we can respond to the changing needs of artists.

The mission of PART
serve artists through
presentation, and th
critical writing, and
into public contexts
screenings, performa
programs.

IPANT INC is to
depth consideration,
ublishing of
introduce this work
ough exhibitions,
:es, and educational

Instant Fame. Charles Atlas, installation view, 2003.

PARTICIPANT INC
95 Rivington Street
New York, New York 10002
212 254 4334
212 254 4141 fax
participantinc.org

Ruby Green is a name made up of two colors. The organization was created to provide a space where emerging and established contemporary artists could exhibit their work, regardless of commercial concerns, for the purpose of exchanging creative ideas.

Participation in the Warhol Initiative has come at a crucial time for our organization. We are hoping to use the Initiative grant to address an increase in general operating needs, and to develop fundraising and strategic plans that will guide our growth. We have already garnered attention and newfound respect among peer cultural organizations and our community just by being associated with the Andy Warhol Foundation for the Visual Arts.

Ruby Green was f
advocate for conte
Nashville. The org
a full spectrum of
art through exhib
public programs,
on work that is int
conceptual in app

nded by a local

porary art in

nization presents

ntemporary visual

ons, events and

th a special focus

disciplinary or

ach.

Our space. Ruby Green Contemporary Art Center.

Ruby Green Contemporary Art Center
514 5th Avenue South
Nashville, Tennessee 37203
615 244 7179
rubygreen.org

Smack Mellon is a Brooklyn-based arts organization whose main objective is to nurture and support underrepresented visual artists in the creation and presentation of new work.

Smack Mellon is in the midst of an exciting period of growth and development. As a result of participating in the Warhol Initiative, we look forward to emerging with a comprehensive strategic plan that will enable us to develop our board and staff, broaden our donor base, and make major capital improvements to our new space.

Smack Mellon provides exhibitic
and access to equipment and tec
of ambitious projects. Its Visual A
creative technology-based proje
and the Artist Studio Program w
to the crisis in availability of aff
and working in New York City.

portunities, studio workspace,

:al assistance for the realization

Exhibition Program focuses on

ıs well as traditional art forms,

ınched in 2000 in response

ble workspace for artists living

Our front door. Smack Mellon.

Smack Mellon Studios
56 Water Street
Brooklyn, New York 11201
718 422 0989
718 947 1225 fax
smackmellon.org

The Soap Factory is dedicated to the production, presentation, and promotion of emerging contemporary practice across the visual arts. Committed to experimentation and risk-taking, The Soap Factory offers audiences a real and immediate experience of the arts, and encourages a wider understanding of and appreciation for artists and their work.

The Soap Factory is already embarking on major changes; we will be doing a feasibility study on our building that will lead to a full development project for the entire 48,000-square foot space. We hope that the Initiative will be able to provide us with the resources, advice and support to ensure that this development process is smooth and successful, transitioning staff from volunteer to full-time, board from managing to governing, and helping us develop the resources to support programming over 12 months, rather than closing over the winter. In 2007 you will see a fully developed space devoted to presenting cutting edge visual culture, with studio space, spaces for artists and audiences to gather along with commercial office space.

The Soap Factory is loca
warehouse that provides
a range of new work. We
been shown, to do what
present the visitor with
experience of art and the

in a former industrial
unique venue to present
n to show what hasn't
t being done, and to
sceral and immediate
e of the artist.

Live Action Set. Art Shanty Projects, Medicine Lake Plymouth, Minnesota, 2005.

The Soap Factory
P.O. Box 581696
Minneapolis, Minnesota 55458
612 623 9176
soapfactory.org

TRANS> is an arts organization that presents and publishes work that addresses key issues in contemporary art. It aims to give critical and historical context to culture and art practices.

TRANS> hopes the Warhol grant will allow us to plan long-term, build a campaign to match funds, develop an engaged and strong board of directors, and create a business plan to strategize financial stability.

The mission of TRA
dialogue among th
the Americas. The o
to the support and c
work by innovative
and artists. Throug
publications, TRANS
art to an internatior

> is to encourage
nany cultures of
inization is devoted
textualization of
itemporary thinkers
xhibitions and
orings cutting-edge
public.

Koo Jeong-α. Solo exhibition, 2003.

Trans>
511 West 25 Street
Suite 502
New York, New York 10001
646 486 0252
transmag.org

Transformer is an arts organization located in Washington, D.C. that connects and promotes emerging artists locally, nationally and internationally.

We anticipate that participation in the Warhol Initiative will bring the stability we need to be a fully thriving, healthy organization. Our long-term goal is for Transformer to substantially support artists in a comprehensive way including offering residencies, grants, honoraria, exhibition opportunities, and other resources.

Transformer is a conduit f
Partnering with artists, cu
cultural entities, Transfor
advocate for emergent exp
seeks to create a strongho
generated by contempora

merging artistic energy.
rs, art spaces and other
serves as a catalyst and
sion in the visual arts. It
or the freedom of thought
rt.

What's Your Thing?. Window installation by Chuck Ramirez, from the *sub-TEXT* exhibition, 2004.

Transformer Incorporated
1404 P Street NW
Washington, DC 20005
202 483 1102
transformergallery.org

Aljira, A Center for Contemporary Art

Art in General

Artists Space

Atlanta Contemporary Art Center

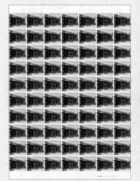

Center for Women & Their Work

CEPA Gallery

Creative Time

Dieu Donné Papermill

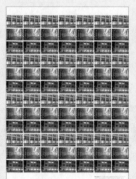

DiverseWorks

Exit Art

509 Cultural Center
aka The Luggage Store

Galería de la Raza

Hallwalls Contemporary Arts Center

Headlands Center for the Arts

Intermedia Arts

Kansas City Artists Coalition

Legion Arts

Los Angeles Contemporary Exhibitions

MACLA/Movimiento de Arte y
Cultura Latino Americana

New Langton Arts

911 Media Arts

Out North

Project Row Houses

Real Art Ways

Salina Art Center

SF Camerawork

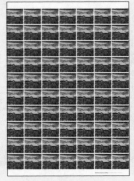

Self-Help Graphics

Southern Exposure

Space One Eleven

SPACES

White Columns

Artspace

Aurora Picture Show

Franklin Art Works

Locust Projects

Midway Contemporary Art

Momenta Art

Participant, Inc.

Ruby Green Contemporary Art Center

Smack Mellon

The Soap Factory

Trans>

Transformer Gallery